Sustainability Economics

D1606167

This book is a concise introduction to an emerging field within economics. Drawing on numerous disciplines, including environmental science, environmental and ecological economics and optimal growth theory, sustainability remains a hazy and complex subject.

The author set out with two objectives: one, to bring some order into the proliferating measures, models and management of sustainability; and two, to facilitate access to a complex inter-disciplinary subject area. The book points to practical ways of assessing and enhancing the long-term environmental and economic sustainability of our economies.

The result is a fully international study that should bridge the gap between disciplines and prove to be an essential guide to anyone interested in one of the most important concepts in the social sciences.

Peter Bartelmus is a Professor at the University of Wuppertal, Germany. He wrote the book as a Visiting Scholar at Columbia University, USA.

Routledge Textbooks in Environmental and Agricultural Economics

1 **The Economics of Agricultural Development, Second Edition**
George W. Norton, Jeffrey Alwang and William A. Masters

2 **Agricultural Marketing**
James Vercammen

3 **Forestry Economics**
John E. Wagner

4 **Agribusiness Management, Fourth Edition**
Jay Akridge, Freddie Barnard, Frank Dooley and John Foltz

5 **Sustainability Economics**
An introduction
Peter Bartelmus

Sustainability Economics
An introduction

Peter Bartelmus
with illustrations by Arik Bartelmus

Routledge
Taylor & Francis Group

LONDON AND NEW YORK

First published 2013
by Routledge
2 Park Square, Milton Park, Abingdon, Oxon OX14 4RN

Simultaneously published in the USA and Canada
by Routledge
711 Third Avenue, New York, NY 10017

Routledge is an imprint of the Taylor & Francis Group, an informa business

© 2013 Peter Bartelmus

The right of Peter Bartelmus to be identified as author of this work has
been asserted by him in accordance with sections 77 and 78 of the Copyright,
Designs and Patent Act 1988.

British Library Cataloguing in Publication Data
A catalogue record for this book is available from the British Library

Library of Congress Cataloging in Publication Data
Bartelmus, Peter.
  Sustainability economics: an introduction/Peter Bartelmus.
  p. cm.
  1. Environmental economics. 2. Sustainable development.
  3. Economic development–Environmental aspects. I. Title.
  HC79.E5B368 2012
  338.9'27–dc23
  2011047099

ISBN: 978-0-415-68682-2 (hbk)
ISBN: 978-0-415-68683-9 (pbk)
ISBN: 978-0-203-11838-2 (ebk)

Typeset in Times New Roman
by Sunrise Setting Ltd

MIX
Paper from
responsible sources
FSC   FSC® C004839
www.fsc.org

Printed and bound in Great Britain by
TJ International Ltd, Padstow, Cornwall

To Little Lea, who will inherit what we leave behind

Contents

List of figures   ix
List of tables   xi
Preface   xiii
Acknowledgements   xvii

1   Introduction   1

PART 1
Ecological sustainability: How much nature do
we need?   11

2   How much nature do we have?   13

3   How much nature do we need? Can we sustain
     its use?   23

4   What should we do about it?   37

PART 2
Economic sustainability: How much for nature?   47

5   What is the value of nature?   49

6   Accounting for economic sustainability   61

7   What should we do about it?   73

8   Bridging the gap: ecological and environmental
     economics   86

PART 3
Sustainable development: What else do we need? 95

9 A cure-all paradigm? 97

10 What should we do about it? 108

11 Some conclusions: What is countable?
What counts? What should we do about it? 119

References 125
Author index 139
Subject index 143
Appendix 149

A syllabus for a short course, including powerpoint slides, can be accessed at the book's web page at www.routledge.com

Figures

1.1	Anthropocentric and eco-centric view of the human environment	2
1.2	Economic exchange system	3
1.3	Environment–economy interaction	3
1.4	Finding the balance	5
1.5	Environmental-economic polarization	7
2.1	Global warming	16
2.2	Ecological Footprint 2007, major world regions	17
2.3	Material flow accounts of the European Union	19
2.4	Global energy balance	20
3.1	How bad is it?	24
3.2	Carrying capacity of people and their activities	25
3.3	Substitution	27
3.4	Economic growth and resource productivity in Germany: an input–outout model	29
3.5	Limits-to-growth model, business-as-usual scenario	30
3.6	Ecological Footprint trend	31
4.1	Delinking natural resource use from economic growth – a tunnel vision?	39
4.2	μηδέν ἄγαν, nothing in excess	41
4.3	Corporate social responsibility	42
4.4	Command and control	43
5.1	The value of nature	50
5.2	Environmental externality	51
5.3	How much for an elephant?	53
5.4	The total economic value	54
5.5	Discounting the damage of a nuclear meltdown	55
5.6	How much for nature? How much for economic output?	57
5.7	Economic values of an environmental service	59
6.1	GPI, GDP and personal consumption per capita, USA, 1950–2004	62

6.2   SEEA: incorporating natural capital in the
      national accounts   64
6.3   Environmentally adjusted net Capital Formation (ECF)
      in world regions   68
7.1   Environmental policy instruments   76
7.2   Optimal eco-tax   77
7.3   Environmental Kuznets curve (EKC), confirmed
      and rejected   79
7.4   Economic discounting   80
7.5   Technology the saviour?   81
7.6   Rent capture and economic growth in Botswana
      and Namibia   82
8.1   Bridging the gap?   87
8.2   Simplified structure of NAMEA   89
8.3   Hybrid input–output model   90
8.4   Linear programming of ecologically sustainable and
      optimal economic activities   92
9.1   Sustainable development – in reductionist mode?   98
9.2   Least and most developed countries according to
      the Human Development Index 2010   98
9.3   The four pillars of sustainable development   99
9.4   Harmony in the clouds – dissent on earth   101
9.5   Sustainable development ranking of selected countries   103
9.6   Globalization is not new   104
10.1 Think globally and act locally?   109
10.2 Eco-techniques   110
10.3 Priorities for sustainable development, the Netherlands 111
10.4 Agenda 21   112
10.5 Deglobalization   114
10.6 Global Compact   115
11.1 Sustainability categories   120
Appendix   Historical perspective of *eco*-nomics   125

Tables

1.1	Schools of *eco*-nomic thought	6
2.1	Environmental indicators of selected countries	15
2.2	Ecological Footprint 2007, selected country rankings and scores	17
3.1	Millennium Development Goal 7, 'environmental sustainability': targets and indicators	32
3.2	Business as usual: how much nature do we need? How much can we expect?	33
5.1	Environmental non-market effects of economic activity and policy	51
5.2	Global cost of climate change	56
6.1	SEEA case study: Germany, 1990	67
7.1	Cost–benefit analysis of deforestation: El Nido, Philippines	74
7.2	Marginal cost of climate change	78
8.1	Physical input–output table, Germany, 1990	88
11.1	Micro- and macro-concepts of sustainability	121

Preface

The apparent rationality of economics has lured scholars into applying economic analysis to almost anything. *Freakonomics*, for instance, claims to reveal 'the hidden side of everything' (Levitt and Dubner 2005). Beyond some clever phrasing the practical results are often disappointing. So, why another book on 'sustainability economics'? Three reasons come to mind. The first is the popular, but cornucopian paradigm of sustainable development: it serves everyone and everything. To industry it offers opportunities for environmental innovation, governments adopt it to pacify environmentalist objections to economic growth, and civil society uses it to argue against globalization. Vague objectives of meeting human needs, increasing well-being or improving the quality of life make sustainable development an alluring notion, for which no one can be held accountable. Sustainability economics trims and quantifies these generic concepts with the help of environmentally modified economic analysis and indicators.

The second reason is a distinct polarization of environmentalists and economists, and more specifically, ecological and environmental economists. Their dissent is about what should primarily be sustained. Ecological economists argue that environmental conservation should get higher priority than economic concerns in a world facing environmental disaster. Environmental economists are more optimistic; they believe in the power of markets and human ingenuity to sustain both the economy and the environment. Sustainability economics reviews the different approaches and reveals possibilities of reconciling or at least connecting the two sides.

The third and probably most important reason is that economics actually applies sustainability in its concepts and models of economic growth. Quite some time ago, Hicks (1939) defined income as 'a guide for prudent conduct' so as to avoid a decline in consumption and well-being. National accountants and modellers of economic growth translated non-decline of income and consumption into maintaining the capital base of economic activity. It is a small logical step to extend the notion of capital maintenance to the use of scarce environmental assets and their services. Economic sustainability is a benchmark against which the prudence of individual behaviour and economic and environmental policies can be tested. It would be the backbone of a new discipline of 'sustainability economics'.

More and more voices, however, especially from business, claim that there is no reason for just sustaining good things like income and consumption when you can have more of them. They also hold that established economic analysis and policy are well equipped to incorporate environmental concerns into efficiently maximized and distributed output, income and ultimately welfare. Sustainability seems to be redundant from this point of view. At the other end of the range of opinions, environmentalists question the relevance of 'puzzle-solving' (Funtowicz and Ravetz 1991) economic models when facing environmental catastrophe. The present book explores possible common or middle ground in these arguments. It focuses on the measurable and comparable, which is the environmental sustainability of economic performance and growth. Narrowly defined sustainability of economic activity stands a better chance of success than holistic visions of development.

The book draws some argumentative power from a previous publication on quantitative methods of environmental and ecological economics (Bartelmus 2008). It goes beyond measurement, though, when exploring the use and usefulness of sustainability concepts advanced by environmentalists and environmental economists. It does not brush over dissent and uncertainty. Rather, it reviews critically the pros and cons of their approaches and attempts to build bridges across the two camps. Admittedly, these bridges are not solid. Hopefully, they can still carry some dialogue on how to combine the different efforts of attaining ecological and economic sustainability.

All this sounds highly complex and difficult, and it is; but the sustainability of our living standards in a safe and healthy environment affects us all. An accessible, yet rigorous, introduction seems to be all the more necessary. I have tried to provide a simple, non-technical narrative, supplemented by annotated suggestions for further reading (the sections titled 'Want to know more?'). Obviously brevity and accessibility come at a price: it is the rather subjective omission or relegation to further reading of topics that might deserve better. Pointed questions at the end of each chapter raise some of these topics, and invite review and discussion.

A concise introduction made easy should appeal to students of economics and the life sciences, who want to look beyond the boundaries of their established coursework. Hopefully it will also reach the governments and civil society, who will once again meet in Rio de Janeiro – this time to address the 'greening' of our economies. They would be well advised to see what fact-based sustainability economics has to say about it.

Parts 1 and 2 of the book describe and compare the main approaches to combining or at least connecting the measurement and analysis of environment and economy. They do this from the points of view of ecological and environmental economics and their sustainability concepts. Part 3 assesses the relevance of the all-encompassing philosophy of sustainable development. In all cases we ask what should and could be sustained, and what we should do about it. Conclusive remarks contend that sustainability economics provides quantifiable benchmarks for prudent economic and environmental behaviour and policy.

Peter Bartelmus
Davao, Philippines
August 2011

Acknowledgements

I wrote this book as a resident scholar at Columbia University; access to its research facilities was invaluable, especially when commuting between the Philippines and New York. My special thanks go to Professor Susan Elmes of the economics department for her kind support of my work. Two anonymous reviewers gave detailed comments and pointed out inconsistencies and generics, of which I am quite critical, myself. It felt good to return to Routledge, whose editors helped efficiently and managed to publish the book in record time. As always, my former colleagues Alessandra Alfieri, Eszter Horvath and Reena Shah of the United Nations Statistics Division kept me up to date on new developments in environment statistics and green accounting. Art and economics collaborated in a particularly rewarding manner when my son Arik Bartelmus created the illustrations; he also showed great patience with my repeated requests for additions and amendments. I am grateful to all of the above.

Permissions to reproduce figures or charts are also gratefully acknowledged. They include those by Stefan Bringezu; Elsevier; Eolss Publishers Co. Ltd; the Intergovernmental Panel on Climate Change; Dennis Meadows; Bernd Meyer; the Netherlands Environmental Assessment Agency; Springer Science+Business Media B.V.; Taylor & Francis; VisLab/Wuppertal Institute for Climate, Environment and Energy.

1   Introduction

What's economics got to do with it?

- *Environment* is all the living and non-living things around us
- *Economy* is the supply and use system of goods and services
- *Environment and economy interact* with good and bad effects for our well-being
- *Environmental economists* rely on adjusting markets and technology to maintain environmental services and economic growth
- *Ecological economists* call for curbs on or changes to economic growth, which they see as the culprit of environmental decline
- *Sustainability economics* encompasses micro- and macro-concerns of sustaining economic growth and development

---

'It' refers to the environment as a key concern of sustaining economic activity and human health and well-being. This first chapter explores the interaction of the environment and the economy as the cause of environmental problems – problems that threaten the lasting supply of both environmental services and economic products. Financial flows of credits and debts may also sustain or undermine economic activity. Purely economic and financial issues are, however, the subject of standard economic analysis and are not further explored here.

Let us first find out what is behind the basic notions of 'environment' and 'economy'. The nineteenth-century German biologist and philosopher Ernst Haeckel (1866: 286) defined ecology as the 'total science of the relationships of the organism with its surrounding outer world'. Replacing 'organism' by 'human beings' gives us a definition of the **human environment**: it includes all of nature, other humans, and human-made goods such as streets, buildings and computers. Different views about the place of humans in their natural environment characterize two basic attitudes towards nature. 'Deep' environmentalists see people as a part of nature, on a par with other living beings. In contrast to this eco-centric view, the more popular anthropocentric view looks for nature's benefits for humans: it sees nature as a provider of services in support of human life and well-being. Figure 1.1 illustrates the two worldviews that gave rise to different schools of thought about human interaction with the natural environment.

Figure 1.2 is a simplified description of the exchange of goods and services in markets. It gives a first impression of what the **economy** is. Households provide work for enterprises, which remunerate labour with wages and salaries. As consumers, households use their income to buy the goods and services produced by enterprises, or they save part of their income for future purchases. More detailed descriptions of economic activity include governmental and non-governmental organizations and financial institutions. The national accounts define these economic agents more rigorously and measure their transactions in units of money. Economic theory attempts to explain and predict the behaviour of economic agents and their effects on the economy.

So what is the problem? The problem is that environment and economy interact, and not always in good ways. Nature sustains life on earth with oxygen, food, water, energy and habitat. It also supplies the economy with natural resources of timber, oil, metals, minerals, livestock and agricultural products. Moreover, nature takes care not only of its own wastes,

(A)   (B)

Figure 1.1 Anthropocentric (A) and eco-centric (B) view of the human environment. View A sees nature as the provider of natural resources and services of recreation and waste disposal. View B rejects the dominance of humans over nature and considers all living things as equal in their rights to life and reproduction.

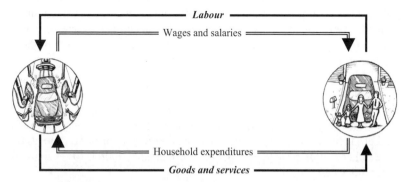

Figure 1.2 Economic exchange system. Enterprises produce goods and services. Households work for enterprises and spend their income on purchases of goods and services.

but also of wastes and pollutants from the economy. On the other hand, natural disasters and overuse of nature's services by humans take a toll on human health and well-being. Figure 1.3 shows nature's services as flows of natural resources from the environment to the economy and back into the

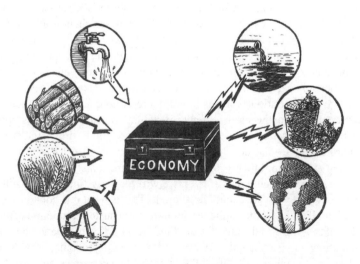

Figure 1.3 Environment–economy interaction. Source functions of supplying natural resources and recreation, and sink functions of absorbing pollutants and wastes are the main environmental services for the economy. Environmentalists often treat the economy as a black box, whose inner workings are largely irrelevant when facing environmental disaster (see Chapter 2).

environment as wastes and emissions. The uses and abuses of environmental services create good and bad effects for human well-being. Economists call the good effects utility and the bad ones disutility or damage, when they refer to individuals. For society or nations, they label the sum of these effects as an increase or decrease of economic welfare.

Nature's capacity for providing environmental services is limited. Environmentalists hold that excessive economic and demographic growth and associated technology destroyed much, if not most, of our natural resources. They see the growth of the human population and its consumption and production patterns as the main cause of **environmental deterioration**. The rather tautological *IPAT* equation (Ehrlich and Holdren 1971) summarizes this view:

$$I = P \times A \times T = P \times \frac{\text{GDP}}{P} \times \frac{I}{\text{GDP}} = I$$

Here I is environmental impact, P is population size, $A = \text{GDP}/P$ is affluence and $T = I/\text{GDP}$ is technological impact.

As discussed in Chapter 3, exponential population growth could bring about a Malthusian decline in welfare. Population growth and concentration in urban areas also overburdens the planet with people's wastes. A 'full world', full of buildings, infrastructure and people and their wastes, is overloading the planet's carrying capacity for humans and their artefacts (Daly 1996). Such a world is likely to collapse* unless we find ways of drastically reducing the use of the natural environment. Mainstream economists doubt that the end is near. They put their faith in human ingenuity and in the power of markets to deal with increasingly scarce environmental services.

Whatever the outlook for our future, there is no question that there are ultimate limits to the earth's funds of natural resources and absorptive sinks for our wastes. The recognition that these limits might undermine economic growth and development is the basic premise for a new field of study – **sustainability economics**. Environmentalists and economists disagree, however, on when, if ever, we will hit these limits, what will be the effects, and what we should do about it. This is what this book is about: to find out if and how the natural environment can sustain economic activity and welfare – now and in the future. Finding an efficient balance between maintaining environmental services and generating income, wealth and welfare is the main objective of sustainability economics (Figure 1.4).

---

* See the 'Want to know more?' section at the end of this chapter. Henceforth all asterisks in the text should be taken to refer to those sections.

Figure 1.4 Finding the balance. Sustainability economics explores synergisms and trade-offs between economic production and consumption and environmental quality.

The emphasis is on efficiency, as it is mostly ignored in advocating sustainable development.

Distinct and often contradictory views about how to assess and tackle environmental problems, and consequently sustainability, are at the origin of different **schools of environmental-economic thought**. Table 1.1 summarizes (and simplifies) these schools under different categories of '*eco*-nomics' (Bartelmus 2008). The four categories show increasing intensity of intervention in the economy for the sake of environmental protection. Conventional (neo-classical) economics seeks income and welfare maximization without considering environmental constraints. Environmental economics accounts for the scarcity of environmental services as an additional cost of otherwise unrestricted economic activities. Ecological economists believe that the dire situation of a full world calls for curbs on or at least radical changes to economic activity; they favour rules and regulations over market instruments to slow down or halt economic growth. Deep ecologists are least concerned about economic scarcity and efficiency; adhering to the egalitarian eco-centric view, they seek a symbiotic relationship with nature. In their view, only a return to lower production, consumption and population levels can save the earth.*

Table 1.1 Schools of *eco*-nomic thought

Conventional economics	Environmental economics	Ecological economics	Deep ecology
- Maximization of profit, utility/ welfare and economic growth - **Unfettered markets** determine production and consumption of goods and services	- Maximization of profit, utility/ welfare and economic growth - **Market intervention** by governments to make economic agents pay for environmental damage	- Reduced, zero or radically altered economic growth - **Collective responsibility and policy** for nature: rules and regulations for the use of environmental services	- Negative growth of economy and population - Restoration of the environment to attain **symbiosis** of humans with nature

Even the less radical environmental and ecological economists adopt different approaches. Figure 1.5 illustrates a distinct **polarization** in dealing with environmental problems and the sustainability of the economy:

- environmental economists cost and budget environmental deterioration (part A) for making economic activity environmentally accountable and sustainable; and
- ecological economists warn us about the non-sustainability of current economic activity, stemming from its physical 'burden' or pressure on the environment (part B).

This book addresses the sustainability of economic performance and development mostly at the national level, with some excursions into local and global issues. However, micro-economic behaviour of households and enterprises is very much part of the picture: this is the case when it comes to explaining and influencing individual preferences for economic and environmental goods and services. To address the interaction of micro- and macro-planning and policy at local, national and international levels a combined approach is chosen, rather than the standard split into micro- and macro-economics. Note also that the crude distinction between ecological and environmental economics serves didactic purposes. Related schools of *eco*-nomics modify and sometimes combine the concepts and methods of the two basic approaches.* The timeline in the Appendix gives a historic overview of the key players responsible for combining environmental and economic analysis. It shows, in particular, the merging of thermodynamic physics and ecology in what became ecological economics,

A. Environmental economics: how much for nature?

B. Ecological economics: how much nature do we need?

Figure 1.5 Environmental-economic polarization. Part A illustrates the monetary analysis of environmental economists; US$ 30 billion is a green accounting estimate of environmental cost in West Germany (see Chapter 6). Part B indicates the physical assessment of environmental impacts by material flow accounts; for industrialized countries the total material burden of natural resource use amounts to about 80 tons per capita per year (see Chapter 2).

Source: © VisLab/Wuppertal Institute for Climate, Environment and Energy, Thomas Poessinger 2001, with permission from the copyright holder.

and the extension of mainstream economics into the use of environmental services, the foundation of environmental economics.

The first two parts of the book explore the fundamental approaches of ecological and environmental economics to sustainability definition, measurement and policy. Part 1 asks how much of nature's biophysical source and sink functions is required to attain ecological sustainability. Part 2 explores the economic and environmental costs and benefits of sustaining economic performance and growth; the results are economic sustainability concepts. Note that the frequently used term 'environmental sustainability' is generally avoided. The reason is that both ecological and economic sustainability seek to maintain the environment. Part 3 wonders what else we need and need to sustain when tackling all-encompassing sustainable development. The overall objective is to evaluate the use and usefulness of these concepts, measures and methods for sustaining both the use of the environment and the productivity of the economy.

Want to know more?

In pre-industrial times Malthus (1798/1963) warned that unfettered exponential population growth would meet with limited supply of food, and populations would be reduced to subsistence level. Similar **doom** emanated from the environmental movement, including predictions of a 'silent spring' (Carson 1965) and the possible collapse of society and economy by transgressions of the 'limits to growth' (Meadows *et al.* 1972, 1992, 2004) (see also Chapter 3). Sceptical voices are Nordhaus (1973), Beckerman (1992) and Lomborg (2001). Critique and counter-critique of Lomborg's scepticism can be found at <www.lomborg-errors.dk> and <www.lomborg.com> (accessed 18 June 2011). The famous Simon–Ehrlich wager illustrates a rather playful debate between environmental doomsayers and doomslayers (AAG Center for Global Geography Education 2011). Hurricanes, floating ice bears and dried out riverbeds evoke Al Gore's 'inconvenient truth' about catastrophic effects of global warming (Gore 2006). In a similar vein, Lovelock (2009) applies his Gaia metaphor to climate change, warning that global warming could make the earth uninhabitable in most places.

Textbooks of **environmental economics** describe the 'internalization' of neglected or ignored environmental costs into the budgets of enterprises and households. The idea is to maintain profit and utility maximization under ideal market conditions (see Chapter 7). Cost–benefit analysis is also usually suggested for choosing among environmental protection programmes (Chapter 7). Clear introductions are, among many others, Turner *et al.* (1993) and Tietenberg (2005). The book by Hanley *et al.* (2007) is a more advanced text for graduate students of economics.

Costanza *et al.* (1997a) gives a concise review of **ecological economics**. A good read, albeit more advocatory in nature, is Daly (1996). Herman Daly is one of the main protagonists of ecological economics. His book is frequently used here for describing environmentalist rejection of mainstream and, to some extent, environmental economics. Bartelmus (2008) compares both schools as part of a broader concept of '*eco*-nomics'. Lawn (2007) follows the tenets of Daly, introducing his 'steady-state' (no-growth) criteria into the analysis of macro-economic equilibrium. Söderbaum (2008) equates sustainability economics with sustainable development, from an ecological economics point of view.

Other schools of *eco*-nomics. Focusing on the polarization of ecological and environmental economics is a simplification. It reduces a variety of approaches to two basic categories, leaning either towards the preservation of nature at all cost, i.e. ignoring cost, or towards the integration of environmental cost into economic accounting and analysis. The Gaia hypothesis (Lovelock 1988/1995), which sees the earth behaving like a living self-regulating organism, is one extreme of largely ignoring economics. At the other end of the range, neo-liberal laissez-faire economics ignores the environment. Among those in-between, we find bio-economists (European Association for Bioeconomic Studies 1997), who seek the symbiotic integration of humans into nature, and industrial ecologists, who look for (natural-resource-saving) eco-efficiency in enterprises (Ayres and Ayres 2002). Co-evolutionary economics (Norgaard 1994) applies the ecological concept of evolution to society, monitoring the change of social values, knowledge, organization and the environment (Chapter 9). Røpke (2005) describes the search of ecological economics for identity versus mainstream economics and ecology. Atkinson *et al.* (2007) take sustainable development as an umbrella for a collection of articles on the sustainability of economic growth and development; they deal with many issues raised in this book.

Points for discussion

- Is Christian faith – 'fill the Earth and subdue it' (Genesis 1: 28) – at the roots of the anthropocentric view of the environment (cf. White 1967)?
- Do the losses of environmental services outweigh the benefits of economic goods and services? Compare your answers to those of Chapters 6 and 7.
- Are human well-being and welfare useful concepts for assessing environmental damages and benefits? Check out the welfare and happiness indicators in Chapter 6.
- What is your gut feeling (or vision): are we heading towards environmental disaster? Revisit this question after each part of the book.
- Pricing the priceless or weighting by weight (Figure 1.4) is one symptom of the polarization of environmental and ecological economists. Do you think – as many environmentalists and economists do – that this antagonism is overstated? See also the attempt at reconciling the two camps in Chapter 8.
- Economics: part of the problem or part of the solution? See how the book answers this question (Chapter 11).

Part 1

Ecological sustainability

How much nature do we need?

2 How much nature do we have?

- *Environmental indicators* warn us about environmental degradation and its welfare effects
- *Global warming* is an important environmental concern but not a surrogate for overall degradation
- *Material flow accounts* measure potential pressures on the environment
- *Energy accounts* use the energy content of materials and products as indicators of efficiency and potential environmental impact
- Material and energy *flows* cannot measure how much nature we have, unless compared to the *funds* of natural resources
- The *Ecological Footprint* relates natural resource consumption to source and sink capacities; controversial 'area equivalents' assess biocapacities
- According to the Ecological Footprint, human *use of the environment exceeds the world's biocapacity* by 50 per cent

How much nature do we have? The answer of deep ecologists, like those of the Gaia school, might be: we do not have any; rather, we are guests on a planet, which we should leave untarnished to the next generation. Quite a number of environmentalists and ecological economists subscribe to this eco-centric view. To them, the real question is: **what have we done to nature?** They see the real world as vandalized and on the edge of disaster:

- The world is in an '"overshoot-and-collapse" mode' (Brown 2006: 5).
- 'Our climate crisis… has become a true *planetary emergency*' (Gore 2006: back cover).
- 'For the first time in history, we face the risk of global decline' (Diamond 2005: 23).

Economic values and preferences do not count much in these cases and may even impede saving the planet (Chapter 3). Figure 1.3 explained this situation as living in a black-box economy that gobbles up nature's goods and spews out wastes and pollutants into the environment. The 'core belief' of ecological economists is that our economies have 'already reached or exceeded the maximum sustainable scale' (Røpke 2005: 267). Much of ecological economics is therefore about providing evidence for actual or looming environmental disaster, and hence the non-sustainability of current economic activity.

Environmental indicators measure the state and trend of the different environmental media of air, water and land.* They warn us about environmental degradation and its effects on human health and well-being. Topics include climate change, natural resource depletion, destructive land use, pollution and natural disasters. To assess these broad areas one has to determine 'representative' indicators. Any list of indicators is therefore bound to be selective and judgemental. Also, the use of different units of measurement makes it difficult to compare indicators and to combine them in an index of overall environmental quality or sustainability. What are we to make of the following indicators, typically advanced as evidence for global environmental non-sustainability of economic and demographic growth (Bartelmus 2008):

- 1.4–5.8°C of global warming by the year 2100;
- a net loss of 7.3 hectares per year of forest cover;
- a loss of 68 species since 1970;
- degradation of 23 per cent of usable land area;
- overexploitation of 27 per cent of fish stocks;
- 40 per cent of the world population facing serious water shortage;
- 5–6 per cent of ozone layer decline in the mid-latitudes of the earth?

Looking at the underlying statistics reveals problems of data availability and quality. Table 2.1 shows data gaps in a United Nations collection of environmental indicators. The table also illustrates the difficulty of evaluating the trend of environmental quality. What does the jumble of happy, indifferent and sad face icons mean for the sustainability of economic activity and human welfare?

The simplest way to get the overall picture is to select an overriding concern and a representative measure. For some time now, **global warming** has been the embodiment of environmental deterioration. But should *one* topic in the limelight overshadow other environmental and social concerns such as deforestation, water shortage, pollution, nuclear energy risks, and

Table 2.1 Environmental indicators of selected countries[a]

	Australia	China	Germany	South Africa	USA
Water					
Freshwater delivered per capita (m^3)	592 (2004)	—	56 (2007)	—	—
Population connected to wastewater collection (%)	87 (2004)	46 (2004)	96 (2007)	60 (2007)	71 (1996)
Air pollution					
SO_2 emission per capita (kg)	125.3	—	6.0	—	33.3
Change in SO_2 emission since 1990 (%)	67 (2008)	—	−91 (2008)	—	−51 (2008)
Climate change					
Greenhouse gas (GHG) emission per capita (t)	26.1	3.4 (1994)	11.7	9.4	22.2
Change in GHG emission since 1990 (%)	31 (2008)	—	−22 (2008)	9 (1994)	13 (2008)
Waste					
Municipal collection per capita (kg)	—	—	587 (2009)	—	736 (2005)
thereof: recycled (%)	30 (2003)	—	47 (2009)	—	24 (2005)
Hazardous waste (Mt)	—	14.3 (2009)	22.3 (2008)	—	34.8 (2005)
Land use					
Change in forest area 1990–2010 (%)	−3	32	3	0	3
Evaluation[b]					
SO_2 emission (since 1990)	☹☹	—	☺☺	—	☺
Water supply to total population (latest year)	☺☺	—	☺☺	☺	☺
GHG emission (since 1990)	☹	—	☺	☹	☹
Hazardous waste (latest year)	☹☹	☹	☹	—	☹☹
Forest area (since 1990)	☺	☺☺	☺	☺	☺

Source: United Nations Statistics Division (2010).

Notes:
a Updated in 2011; year of compilation in parentheses.
b According to colour codes in maps.

poverty (Figure 2.1)? Even if we accept average temperature increase as the environmental measure, it is less clear how it will affect human well-being, and where and when (Chapter 5). The most authoritative assessment puts global warming by the end of the century at between 1.8°C and 4.0°C (Intergovernmental Panel on Climate Change (IPCC 2007a). The same report also gives 'likely' estimates of decreasing snow cover and sea ice,

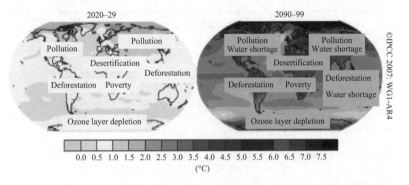

Figure 2.1 Global warming. Projected temperature increase in the twenty-first century (comparing the third to the last decade). Global warming may obscure other environmental and social concerns.

Source: Adapted from IPCC (2007a, Figure SPM.6).

increasing sea levels and tropical cyclones, and increasing and decreasing precipitation in different parts of the planet. These are hardly accurate measures of the state of the environment or environmental sustainability, even if one cannot deny the potential severity of global warming. A balanced assessment should see climate change in the context of other environmental and socio-economic concerns. Comprehensive physical and monetary indices and accounts claim to provide this context. This chapter discusses briefly selected biophysical assessments; Chapter 6 presents the monetary approaches.

   The **Ecological Footprint** measures demand for, and hence pressure on, bioproductive land and water from the use of renewable natural resources and wastes. Demand is expressed as the 'area required to produce all the resources an individual, population, or activity consumes, and to absorb the waste they generate' (Ewing *et al.* 2010: 8). Further analysis compares the Footprint to nature's supply of 'biocapacity' or area available for resource use and waste absorption. The result is a measure of ecological deficit, if a nation exceeds nature's capacity of providing environmental services, or an ecological credit, if it keeps some unused capacity for potential services. The implicit idea is to assess the sustainability of using environmental services, taking limits in their availability into account. Calculations for 2007 present an average of 1.8 ha of biocapacity available per person on earth and an average footprint of 2.7 ha. The world thus faces an ecological deficit of 50 per cent of its biocapacity. Figure 2.2 shows the footprints and resulting ecological deficits or credits for major world regions.

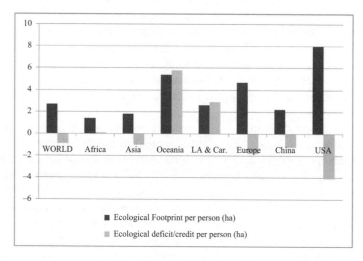

Figure 2.2 Ecological Footprint 2007, major world regions. The world exceeded its available biocapacity of 18 billion hectares (1.8 ha per person) by an ecological deficit of over 6 billion ha (0.9 ha per person). The USA generated one of the world's highest footprints of 8 ha per person. Free biocapacity in Oceania and Latin America exceeds the footprint of these regions.

Source: Ewing *et al.* (2010).

Table 2.2 presents selected national footprint scores and rankings. The USA is second, surpassed only by the United Arab Emirates, with each person using 8 ha of nature on an average. People in poor countries generate much lower footprints than rich ones. Obviously, the production and

Table 2.2 Ecological Footprint 2007, selected country rankings and scores

Country	Rank	Score (ha per capita)	Deficit/credit (ha per capita)
United Arab Emirates	152	10.7	−9.8
USA	148	8.0	−4.1
Sweden	140	5.9	3.9
United Kingdom	122	4.9	−3.6
Russia	113	4.4	1.3
Brazil	97	2.9	6.1
China	79	2.2	−1.2
Iraq	42	1.4	−1.1
Philippines	38	1.3	−0.7
Kenya	28	1.1	−0.5
Timor-Leste	1	0.4	0.8

Source: Ewing *et al.* (2010).

consumption levels and techniques of industrialized countries require more natural resource inputs and generate correspondingly higher waste and pollution. Depending on the available biocapacity, the level of foot-prints does not necessarily correlate with the levels of ecological deficits or credits. Sweden and the United Kingdom have similar footprints. But different endowment with environmental services makes Sweden an ecological creditor, whereas the UK's footprint exceeds the use of the country's biocapacity.

The Ecological Footprint calculates national biocapacities by applying a global area equivalent (per capita average) to a country's population. Responding to criticism that this ignores the possibility of importing biocapacity from other countries, the latest Footprint version now includes the footprints of imported and exported commodities. Other improvements are an open discussion of calculation and interpretation problems, notably the omission of non-renewable resources and wastes. Most of these impacts are not related to biological capacities and could thus be excluded from an 'ecological' measure. Still, one important issue remains: the conversion of potential environmental impacts into area equivalents. Such conversion into a common unit of measurement allows different pressures to be summed into one footprint index. To this end, 'equivalent factors' estimate the bioproductive area required for food and wood production, urbanization and the absorption of carbon from CO_2 emissions. Hectares are poor measures, though, of widely differing resource uses and pollutants, and of actual impacts of environmental depletion and degradation.

Physical laws of conservation of energy and matter and their after-use dispersal support more 'balanced' measurement. **Material flow accounts** calculate the mass (in units of weight) of material inputs into the economy as equal to the mass of materials staying in the economy or released as wastes and pollutants.* Figure 2.3 shows the material flow account of the European Union. The account records in principle all natural resource flows into the economy of the EU, including those contained in imports, and their final discharges as 'residuals' into the environment and non-EU countries. The key measure of Total Material Input is also called Total Material Requirement because it includes unused materials of earth and biomass moved and disposed in construction, mining and agriculture. These 'hidden flows' (Eurostat 2001: 15) are also part of the solid wastes of Total Material Output. Water use is excluded because of its relative magnitude, which would 'drown out' all other material flows. In industrialized countries, Total Material Requirement appears to converge to an annual 80 tonnes per capita. Japan's 40 tonnes is an exception, reflecting its low energy consumption (Bringezu 2002).

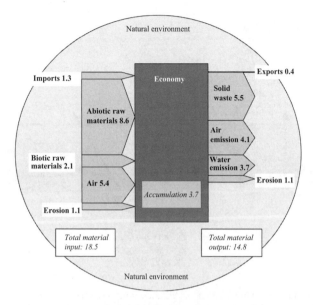

Figure 2.3 Material flow account of the European Union (EU-15, 1996). The total mass of primary material inputs (18.5 billion tonnes (Gt)) equals the mass of accumulation of materials in the economy (3.7 Gt) plus total material outputs of wastes and emissions (14.8 Gt). Material flow accounts still treat the economy as a black box (cf. Figure 1.3), except for some accumulation of materials.

Source: Bringezu (2002), with permission from the copyright holder S. Bringezu.

Energy accounts could be an alternative to material flow accounts. This would be the case if one could employ energy values as a common measuring rod for material inputs into and residual outputs from economic activities. Energy economists and accountants claim that economic products and their environmental impacts of natural resource depletion and pollution can indeed be valued by their energy content. They also believe that the availability of useful energy ('exergy') is an indicator of sustainability, since all life on earth depends ultimately on energy (Slesser 1975; Costanza 1980).*

At the planetary level, solar energy inflows and energy outflows can be directly measured in watts or joules (Figures 2.4). Global energy balances reveal the build-up of greenhouse gases that have caused global warming since the beginning of the industrial revolution in the eighteenth century. Measurement problems increase for tracing energy uses and their emissions down to the different production and consumption processes. The reason is the difficulty of obtaining reliable data on the exergy content of

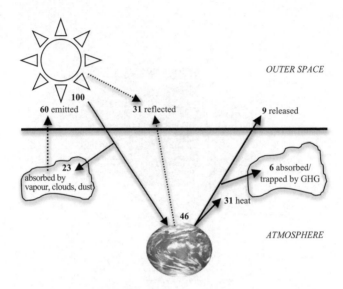

Figure 2.4 Global energy balance. All incoming solar energy (100 per cent) is returned to outer space by emitting 60 per cent (of previously absorbed radiation) from clouds and vapour, reflecting 31 per cent immediately from the earth, and releasing 9 per cent from earth after absorption. Another balance generates the equilibrium temperature on earth of about 27°C by absorbing 46 per cent of the incoming solar energy and releasing it to outer space (9 per cent), into the atmosphere as heat (31 per cent), and absorbing the remainder in clouds, vapour and greenhouse gases (GHG) (6 per cent). The trapping of heat by GHG, in particular CO_2 and methane, is responsible for the greenhouse effect that keeps the earth's temperature at a comfortable level. Increasing GHG emission from human production and consumption is responsible for pushing up the equilibrium temperature, causing global warming and its environmental impacts.

Source: US National Weather Service (2010).

energy carriers such as oil, gas or wood, and also of minerals, metals and pollutants.

All in all, material flow accounts are more practical than footprint calculations and energy accounts. They measure material inputs and outputs directly by their weight and do not require estimates of the energy content or area equivalent of natural resources and residuals. Ignoring, however, the stocks of natural resources they cannot answer the question of how much nature we have. Moreover, the weight of different flows of raw materials (e.g. gold and timber) and pollutants does not measure natural resource depletion and environmental degradation, nor can it reflect their significance for humans and nature. Material input and output indicators show potential pressure only on the environment. The question is how much pressure a country or the planet can endure, i.e. at what level material inputs and outputs become non-sustainable. The next chapter will address this question.

Want to know more?

Combining different environmental impacts into one measure of overall environmental quality or sustainability poses difficult aggregation problems. Most governments and international organizations, therefore, still use indicator *sets*. Conceptual frameworks define scope and coverage and bring some order to long lists of **environmental and sustainable development indicators**. Perhaps best known is the pressure-state-response framework (United Nations 1984; OECD 1993) and its derivatives (United Nations 1996; European Environment Agency, n.d.). However, frameworks and even relatively short 'core' sets of indicators (United Nations 2001; OECD 2003; European Environment Agency 2005) do not capture overall environmental quality and the sustainability of economic activity. Emotional face icons (or colour codes) seek to summarize indicator results (European Environment Agency 2002: 16, 2010: 18–19). Links to international targets such as the Millennium Development Goals (Chapter 9) help, but are subjective and still a far cry from an overall measure of environmental sustainability.

Material flow accounts were developed and applied in Europe (Steurer 1992; Bringezu 1993; Eurostat 2001). They are grounded in thermodynamic laws of energy conservation and dissipation, extended to material flows (Georgescu-Roegen 1979). This extension assumes that the use of matter follows laws of conservation and dispersal similar to those of energy use. The Sustainable Europe Research Institute (SERI 2011) maintains a database of material flows in countries. The OECD (2008) has now adopted material flow accounting, introducing it in the international System of integrated Environmental and Economic Accounts (Chapter 6).

Energy accounts assess the efficiency of energy use in production and consumption. To this end, they defined exergy as the potential useful energy available for doing work (Szargut 2005; Wall 2008). Several articles in the *Encyclopedia of Life Support Systems* (Tolba 2001) discuss exergy accounting for measuring the sustainability of energy use and residual exergy in pollutants. More ambitious 'emergy' accounts measure the total, directly and indirectly embodied, energy in products and energy carriers for similar purposes (Odum 1996, 2002; Brown and Ulgiati 1999). The difficulty of comprehensive accounting for the energy value of all material inputs and residuals prevented energy accounting from becoming as popular as the easier-to-measure material flow accounts.

Points for discussion

- How bad is it? Do environmental and sustainable development indicators show the non-sustainability of our economies? Do they tell us what sustainability is?
- Is climate change an 'inconvenient truth' of impending disaster or a conveniently hyped-up exaggeration of potential environmental hazards? See what Chapter 5 says about the costs of climate change.
- Can we take global warming as a proxy measure of environmental degradation?
- What do the indices tell us? Is exceeding the world's biocapacity a measure of unsustainable demographic and economic growth? Or is this the message of the input and output indicators of the material flow accounts?
- What does the earth's energy balance tell us?
- What are the uses of material flow and energy accounts? How do they compare in measuring environmental impact?
- How much nature do we have? Can we know? Do we need to know?

3 How much nature do we need?

Can we sustain its use?

- Some deep ecologists believe that *nature's own values* of survival and reproduction – rather than human bias – should determine the use of environmental services
- Energy economists and accountants contend that nature invests energy into anything, determining the value of any thing
- *Ecological sustainability* refers to the carrying capacity of people in a territory and the resilience of ecosystems to human perturbations
- *Strong sustainability* requires the preservation of critical natural capital
- Differing results of modelling suggest that *we do not know how much nature we need*

Chapter 2 examined indicators and physical accounts which claim to measure the non-sustainability of economic activity. Perhaps surprisingly, they did not come up with a clear red line or threshold which would separate sustainability from non-sustainability. At first blush, the Ecological Footprint looks like an exception, indicating exceedances of – unfortunately rather murky – biocapacity levels. This chapter attempts to find out more about the sustainability notions that do or should underlie the measurement of sustainability. Asking how much pressure and impact we can endure addresses the minimum requirement for sustaining our standards of living and ultimately well-being.

Our need for nature's services depends on (1) how much nature we will have and (2) how much we value nature. The first question is a matter of prediction, which depends on how much nature we had and have, as discussed in Chapter 2. The second question is a matter of evaluation, either by individual preferences or by the norms and standards of experts, government and non-governmental organizations (Figure 3.1). Both questions combine

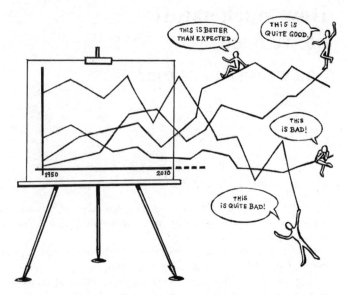

Figure 3.1 How bad is it? Evaluating the trends of environmental impacts requires
modelling future trends and assessing their effects on the economy and
human welfare. Agreement on widely differing results and their interpretation remains elusive.

in definitions and measures of the sustainability of human needs and
wants. Part 2 will explore how markets and market prices reveal individual
preferences for products and nature's services. Here, we look into more
judgemental evaluations by those who are 'in the know'.

Most ecological economists reject the 'commodification' and pricing of
nature. Their vision of (non-)sustainability sees the economy as an expanding component or 'subsystem' of a 'finite and non-growing ecosystem' (Daly
1996: 27). As we saw in the preceding chapters, in their view, the economic
expansion has now reached the limits of the global ecosystem, threatening
all life on earth. In this case, **nature's own values** of survival and reproduction, rather than 'human bias' towards maximizing utility, should rule the
use of nature (Brown and Ulgiati 1999). Energy economists and accountants contend that energy flows can assess both nature's and the economy's
values since energy is a requirement for all processes and activities on earth
(Chapter 2). Nature invests energy into anything, determining the value of
any thing. Problems of converting matter and different energy sources into a
common energy unit and the rejection of human preferences prevented wide
acceptance and application of energy valuation and accounting.

More pragmatic ecological economists let humans back into the picture by exploring how many people a territory (ecosystem, country, the planet) can sustain. This provides us with an **ecological sustainability** concept in the form of a region's carrying capacity (Figure 3.2). On the one hand, carrying capacity depends on the provision of ecosystem services. Besides environmental source and sink functions, these services include life support and recreation, as well as aesthetic and cultural values of nature. On the other hand, carrying capacity also depends on people's needs and wants that are usually expressed as their standards of living. Human efforts to meet desirable standards of living have been the cause of overuse and abuse of ecosystem services. Ecological economists often equate, therefore, ecological sustainability with ecosystem resilience to human disturbances of ecosystem equilibrium (Perrings 1995, 2006). Safe minimum standards are to keep the use of ecosystem services within the boundaries of resilience (Chapter 4).

The two definitions of ecological sustainability reflect different views of what should be sustained. Is it the health or quality of the natural environment, free of biased human preferences, or is it the health and quality of life of humans? Or is it both, with an implicit but fuzzy reasoning of 'what's good for nature is also good for humans'? Ecological economists seem to follow the last argument when proclaiming the need for preserving

Figure 3.2 Carrying capacity of people and their activities. The ecological sustainability of a region is the number of people the region's ecosystems can sustain at a minimum standard of living.

critical natural capital. Criticality of capital refers indeed to both the maintenance of environmental quality and the sustainability of economic production and consumption. Critical natural capital is seen as vulnerable and irreplaceable, and its depletion as irreversible.*

The meaning of irreversibility blurs, however, in the light of counteracting actions and processes that are themselves difficult to pin down, including:

- natural renewal of regrowing biological resources and replenishment of circulating ones like groundwater;
- restoration by investing in the repair or renewal of natural capital;
- substitution of non-renewable and non-restorable natural resources such as minerals or fossil fuels by renewable or reproducible ones;
- discovery of natural resource stocks such as oil or gas deposits.

The distinction of renewable and non-renewable resources is ambiguous, since prolonged overuse of renewables – beyond their maximum sustainable yield* – makes them exhaustible. Uncontrolled access to renewable resources such as fish in the ocean or timber and species in the wilderness has given rise to the 'tragedy of the commons': ignorance about sustainable use brought about resource depletion and loss of livelihood.* Moreover, restoration efforts tend to become impractical and may well be abandoned when facing prohibitive costs of rebuilding complex ecosystems (Coastal Service Center, NOAA n.d.). Substitution may be possible for particular uses of a natural resource like water for swimming; it could fail if other features, for example of an unspoilt seaside, are taken into account (Figure 3.3). It is an open question whether technological progress (Chapter 7) can find a way around using irreplaceable resources. Discovery and improved mining techniques have extended the lifetime of exhaustible resources, much to the surprise of both economists and environmentalists.

Still, ecological economists call for the full preservation of critical natural capital as a **strong sustainability** objective. Advocates of strong sustainability tend to play down the roles of renewability, discovery, restoration and substitution – in a world that is unwilling to refrain from overconsumption of natural resources or unable to invest significantly in their restoration. They also point out that substitution of irreplaceable critical natural capital is not possible by definition, at least with current knowledge and technology (Costanza *et al.* 1991; Daly 1996). In contrast, environmental economists focus on the income-spinning capacity of capital and its potential for generating economic welfare. This capacity permits placing a monetary value on any type of capital, whether natural or produced. Maintaining this value, rather than preserving a particular amount of critical natural capital, is the objective of a weak sustainability concept

Figure 3.3 Substitution. Can we replace polluted beaches with clean swimming pools?

(Chapter 6). The strength of sustainability is a distinctive and distinguishing feature of ecological and environmental economics.

The indicators of the **material flow accounts** cater to relatively strong sustainability; they allow substitution only among different primary raw materials, ignoring possible substitution by other production factors. Material flow indicators do not, however, show how much nature we have and how much of it we have used sustainably or unsustainably. The reason is that the accounts fail to identify the use of critical natural resources and to link the flows of natural resources to resource stocks (Chapter 2). The question then remains: by how much do we have to reduce the inflow of materials from the environment to attain sustainability? The answer is left to the judgement of experts. Perhaps best known is the Factor 4 rule of halving material input while allowing economic output (GDP) to double over the next 20–30 years. Innovative resource-saving technology supposedly obtains a four-fold increase in natural resource productivity, i.e. GDP per unit of material input (von Weizsäcker *et al.* 1997). There is little justification for setting the Factor 4 standard, except for the 'belief' that it 'can put the Earth back into balance' (von Weizsäcker *et al.* 1997: xv).

An **input–output model** attempted to assess the material requirements of the German economy (Meyer 2005). Figure 3.4 indicates some improvement in resource productivity. However, the model shows also that business as usual will not attain the German government's Factor 2.5 target, let alone Factor 4. At the same time, the figure reveals the limitations of looking into the future: the 2008–9 global economic downturn obviously derailed the predictions of continuing GDP growth and corresponding material requirements.

Modelling problems multiply at the global level and by looking further ahead to the end of the century. The popular ***Limits to Growth* report** has therefore met with strong criticism. Its complex simulations predict social collapse if current demographic and economic trends continue.* The report addresses both prediction of environmental impact and evaluation in terms of human welfare. An approximation of the Ecological Footprint represents environmental impact. The Human Development Index (UNDP 2010) supposedly measures welfare as an average of literacy, gross national income per capita and life expectancy.

Figure 3.5 shows the business-as-usual scenario for both indices. Natural resource depletion triggers the downturn of economic output, including food and health services that cause the decline of human welfare. By the end of the century, society's collapse would take the shape of a return to year-1900 standards of living. Non-sustainability in terms of declining welfare could begin in the near future, just before the turning point of environmental impact, brought about by negative demographic and economic growth. The authors hasten to explain that the business-as-usual scenario is not necessarily the most likely outcome since it reflects past behaviour. Individual and governmental reactions to looming disaster might change the outcome as shown in other scenarios. Still, critical voices doubt the validity of the data-poor model and question the underlying exponential growth assumptions.*

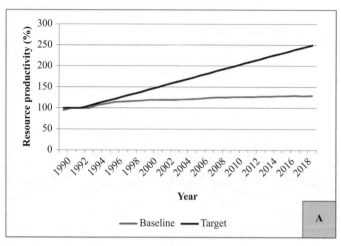

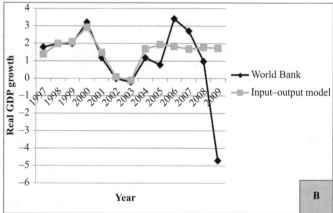

Figure 3.4 Economic growth and resource productivity in Germany: an input–output model. Part A shows that resource productivity (GDP per Total Material Requirement) will increase in the baseline (business-as-usual) scenario of the input–output model from an index level of 100 in the early 1990s to 130 in 2020. This increase by a factor of 1.3 is a far cry from the governmental Factor 2.5 target. Part B illustrates the problems of prediction, comparing the results of actual with modelled GDP growth: note the effect of the 2008–09 recession.

Sources: Input–output model: Meyer (2005), with permission from the copyright holder B. Meyer; World Bank, actual data: World Bank (2011).

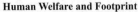

Human Welfare and Footprint

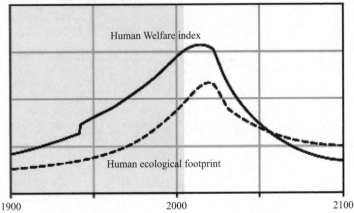

Figure 3.5 Limits-to-growth model, business-as-usual scenario. Human welfare and environmental impact (Ecological Footprint) increase up to a turning point in the first half of the twenty-first century. By the year 2100 human welfare might reach a year-1900 level, with environmental impacts at the level of the 1970s.

Source: Meadows *et al.* (2004: 169, scenario 1), with permission from the copyright holder D. Meadows.

The **Ecological Footprint** aims to show the average per-capita territorial use of the environment (Chapter 2). One could therefore see the Footprint as an inverse measure of carrying capacity. Currently, the Footprint calculations are the only attempt to recurrently measure ecological sustainability at different regional (local, national and global) levels. Future sustainability has to be predicted. Figure 3.6 presents trend extrapolations of the global footprint. According to World Wide Fund for Nature *et al.* (2010), the trend is based on international projections of population, land use, land productivity, energy use, diet and climate change. If business as usual continues, we will overshoot the available biocapacity by 100 per cent in the 2030s. In other words, we will need another planet to meet the needs of our current lifestyles. By 2050, the business-as-usual scenario shows the need for two more planets.

As we are unlikely to colonize other planets anytime soon, it looks like we have to reduce our consumption of nature's services to the available 18 billion hectares of biocapacity (Chapter 2). Yet, we have been overshooting this capacity since the 1980s without causing a major planetary disaster. Can we expect to do so in the future? Or will nature and society collapse? When? World Wide Fund for Nature *et al.* (2010: 86) state laconically that

Number of
additional planets

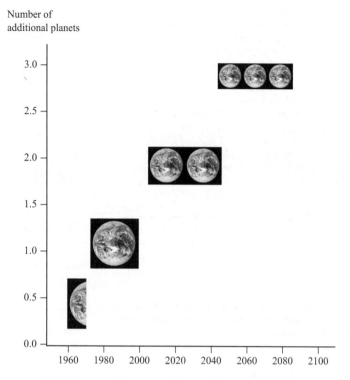

Figure 3.6 Ecological Footprint trend. With business as usual and continuing population growth, we might need two planets in the 2030s and three planets
in the 2070s to maintain our lifestyles.

Source: Until 2050: World Wide Fund for Nature *et al.* (2010); three-planet projection: own
linear extrapolation.

'our present track is unsustainable', but changing the assumptions about
energy use and diet would make the 'development of the world' more
sustainable.

Assumptive and data-poor modelling of the far-away future may be the
reason for more definite but also more judgemental statements about how
much nature we should use. Table 3.1 presents indicators for the different targets of the 'environmental sustainability' goal of the United Nations
Millennium Development Goals (Chapter 9). With the exception of ozone
depletion, the prospects for reaching the targets within the prescribed time
frames do not look good. The political selection of targets and the difficulty
of finding and comparing appropriate indicators make this a questionable
assessment of global sustainability.

Table 3.1 Millennium Development Goal 7, 'environmental sustainability': targets and indicators[a]

Environmental sustainability

Target 7A: Reverse the loss of environmental resources

	2000	2006–10
Forest cover (% of land area)	31.4	31.0[b]
CO_2 emission (billion tons)	24.0	30.0[c]
Ozone depleting substances (million tons)		
Consumption of developing regions	212.5	44.7[d]
Consumption of developed regions	24.1	−1.8[de]
Fish stocks (% within safe biological limits)	72	72[f]
Water resources used (% of renewable water)[g]		
Developing regions	6.7	
Developed regions	9.3	

Target 7B: Reduce significantly biodiversity loss by 2010

	1994/96	2008
Species not expected to go extinct in the near future (% of total number of species)		85.3
Birds	93.5[h]	93.1
Mammals	86.0[i]	85.3

Target 7C: Halve by 2015 the proportion of people without sustainable access to safe drinking water and basic sanitation

	1990	2008
Population using improved drinking water services (% of total population)	77	87
Population using an improved sanitation facility (% of total population)	54	61

Target 7D: By 2020, to have achieved a significant improvement in the lives of at least 100 million slum dwellers

	2000	2010
Urban population of developing countries living in slums (million)	39.3	32.7

Source: United Nations (2010b).

Notes:
a Unless otherwise stated: world figures.
b Year 2010.
c Year 2007.
d Year 2008.
e Exports plus destruction exceed consumption (production plus imports).
f Year 2006.
g Around year 2000.
h Year 1994.
i Year 1996.

Chapter 2 revealed the problems of using environmental impacts of the past as indicators of potential non-sustainability. This chapter defined ecological sustainability more succinctly by extending the sustainability analysis into the future. Table 3.2 illustrates with a few examples the large variety of different sustainability **models and their assumptions**. One type of assumption is the particular set of environmental targets or limits chosen for economic activity. As discussed, standards, targets or rules for limiting the use of environmental services are crucial to the definition and assessment of ecological sustainability. Unfortunately, there is no consensus on

Table 3.2 Business as usual: how much nature do we need? How much can we expect?

Measure/model		Results	Limits/targets	Assumptions
Ecological Footprint		Now: $1\frac{1}{2}$ planets 2030s: 2 planets 2070s: 3 planets	Biocapacity of regions and the globe	Area equivalents for the use of natural resources Linear extrapolation of Ecological Footprint trend
Limits to growth model	*Ecological Footprint*	2020s: maximum footprint 2100: footprint at 1970s level	Availability of natural resource stocks Carrying capacities	Exponential demographic and economic growth
	Welfare Index	Now: declining welfare 2100: welfare at 1900 level		Powerless technology and markets
Total material requirement (input–output model, Germany)		2100: Factor 1.3 of 1992 resource productivity	Factor 2.5: government target Factor 4: non-governmental target	Cost-pushed price setting and technological change Stable economic growth after 2005
Millennium Development Goal: 'environmental sustainability'		As of 2008 Target for ozone depletion reached Meeting other targets: unlikely	United Nations targets and time schedules for environmental sustainability	Politically negotiated targets represent the collective will of nations

environmental limits, whether assessed at local, national or global levels. The question is indeed whether politically negotiated or 'expertly' set targets and standards reflect collective will or the agendas of politicians and the environmental lobby.

Hardly comparable results come as no surprise. By the end of this century:

- we might need a couple of planets;
- human welfare could be at the level of a century ago, although with drastically reduced environmental impacts;
- a dematerialized world economy is unlikely;
- most of the Millennium Development Goals of the United Nations might be as unattainable as those of the preceding Development Decades (Chapter 9).

We might not know how much nature we need to gain ecological sustainability, but ignorance is neither bliss nor a release from responsibility. So what should we do about it? This is the question for the next chapter.

Want to know more?

Ecosystems and ecosystem services play a central role in ecological economics. The interaction of living organisms with their non-living environment characterizes ecosystems. Ecosystems seek to maintain a relatively stable equilibrium for their populations and their metabolism (e.g. Odum 1971). Human skill and technology have the power to overcome the resilience of ecosystems to disturbances of their equilibrium. A big disturbance or shock can lead to a new acceptable equilibrium, or an unacceptable one that might drastically impair the welfare of human populations (Brand 2009). The Millennium Ecosystem Assessment (2005: v) defines ecosystem services as 'benefits people obtain from ecosystems'. Such definition opens the door to a myriad of nature's goods and services which humans could and do use, or might just cherish, such as popular species.

Ecological economists define **critical natural capital** as those parts of the natural environment that perform important and irreplaceable ecological functions (de Groot *et al.* 2003). These functions contribute significantly to welfare and are deemed essential for attaining ecological sustainability (Ekins *et al.* 2003). Sustainability standards and indicators make the generic criteria of criticality (importance and vulnerability/ resilience of natural capital) more operational (de Groot *et al.* 2003; Brand 2009). A special issue of *Ecological Economics* (44, 2003) describes the outcomes of a European research project on critical natural capital and strong sustainability. Vague definitions of natural capital and its criticality make the concept little more than a reminder of threats to ecological sustainability.

Natural growth of a population in an ecosystem such as fish in a well-defined fishing ground typically follows a logistic curve. The population grows rapidly at low stock levels as it has ample resources and space. At some higher level, food scarcity and habitat limitations slow down the growth rate up to a point where it begins to decrease. The turning point of the maximum growth rate also marks the **maximum sustainable yield** or surplus that can be continuously harvested without a decrease in the (fish) population. Any higher and prolonged harvesting rate will lead to a decline and ultimate depletion of the resource. Eventually the ecological constraints of the ecosystem will halt the natural growth of the population at the system's carrying capacity. A vivid description of the sustainable yield model and its limitations can be found in Paterson (2008).

Profit-seeking fishing fleets often exploited renewable resources beyond sustainability levels. The reasons were ignorance or disregard of the risk of triggering depletion, even before reaching maximum sustainable yield. This unintended decline of a natural resource has become known as the **tragedy of the commons** (Hardin 1968). To some extent 'commons' is a misnomer since most traditional communities have managed their common property resources sustainably. 'Open-access resource' is a better term for renewable resources at risk of depletion in situations of uncontrolled exploitation (Turner *et al.* 1993). Fish in the oceans, timber in tropical forests and sinks for pollutants in the atmosphere are resources where governments or other economic agents did not have or did not claim ownership and exploitation rights.

The first *Limits to Growth* **report** created a heated debate with its Malthusian prediction that 'the limits to growth on this planet will be reached sometime within the next 100 years. The most probable result will be a rather sudden and uncontrollable decline in both population and industrial capacity' (Meadows *et al.* 1972: 29). The latest report

(Meadows *et al.* 2004) confirms this prediction. The authors present, however, alternative scenarios with progressively positive results. In the most optimistic scenario, natural resource savings, environmental protection and zero demographic and economic growth create, in 2100, a slight increase in human welfare with a stable and sustainable ecological footprint. Critique refers to (1) assumptions of exponential demographic and economic growth and corresponding environmental impacts, (2) insufficient data, and (3) ignoring market forces, technological progress and changes in social values (Cole *et al.* 1973; Nordhaus 1973; Beckerman 1992). The *Limits to Growth* authors defended their approach in Cole *et al.* (1973).

Points for discussion

- Does carrying capacity, the measure of ecological sustainability, reflect our preferences for environmental and economic goods and services?
- Should nature's values – what are they? – override human values?
- What does ecological sustainability sustain: nature, welfare, the economy?
- Do the predictions of exceeding the biocapacity of earth and of the limits to economic growth confirm your 'gut feelings' (cf. Chapter 1) about pending disaster? Do linear trend extrapolations predict future ecological footprints?
- Are 'expertocratic' or political goals and targets, such as the Millennium Development Goals or dematerialization factors, valid indicators of how much nature should be available for sustainable use?
- How do we know that some assets and amenities of nature are in critical condition? Critical for what? How critical?
- What is the difference between common-property and open-access resources?
- Is technology the saviour (cf. Chapter 7)? How realistic is the Factor 4 suggestion that halving material inputs will make economic growth sustainable?
- How much nature do we need? Can we know? Do we need to know?

4 What should we do about it?

- *Environmental management* rules are principles of the sustainable use of environmental services; adaptive management deals with uncertainty in managing ecosystems
- Measures and models of non-sustainability provide differing and often contradictory *policy* advice
- *Sufficiency* in consumption and *eco-efficiency* in production are micro-economic strategies of ecological sustainability
- *Corporate social responsibility* caters to demands of stakeholders
- *Standards, rules and regulations* are the preferred policy tools of ecological economics
- *Delinking environmental impacts from economic growth* is the macro-economic strategy of ecological sustainability
- *Ecological economics needs a framework* for integrative economic-environmental analysis and policy

Not knowing how much nature we need is not a good start for formulating sustainability policies. Ecological **management rules** or principles are a first response to perceived non-sustainability (Daly 1990; Sachs *et al.* 1998; Lawn 2007). The rules call for:

- the use of renewable resources within their regenerative capacity;
- the use of non-renewable resources as far as their consumption is offset by investing in renewable substitutes;
- the discharge of wastes and residuals without exceeding the absorptive capacities of natural sinks;
- the preservation or restoration of critical natural capital.

The rules refer to the mitigating actions and processes discussed in Chapter 3. Their application faces uncertainty and disagreement about the availability and use of natural resources and ecological services. To what extent should one preserve natural resources, even critical ones, for which future generations might have little use? Are temporary exceedances of source and sink capacities justified if it allows basic needs in poor countries to be met? According to the **precautionary principle** of the Rio Summit, the 'lack of full scientific certainty' in these cases is not 'a reason for postponing cost-effective measures to prevent environmental degradation' (United Nations 1993: Principle 15) – simply stated: better safe than sorry!

One response to this admonition is the setting of safe minimum standards that could avert serious degradation within the bounds of ecosystem resilience.* However, the large variety of ecosystems and their services make it difficult to apply common standards to large territories such as countries or the planet. In practice, ecological sustainability has therefore mostly been applied to the management of particular ecosystems and local agricultural areas. The objective of iterative **adaptive management** (Holling 1978) is to deal with uncertainty in ecosystem use, conservation and restoration. The idea is 'learning by doing and adapting to what is learned' (US Department of the Interior 2010).

For national or international policy, we can examine the **policy recommendations** raised in connection with the measures and models of Chapter 3. In line with the definition of ecological sustainability, they refer to nature's limited carrying capacities or potential pressures on these capacities (Table 3.2).

The authors of the limits-to-growth model provide generic advice: 'Visioning, networking, truth-telling, learning and loving' is to bring about a 'sustainability revolution' (Meadows *et al.* 2004: 269). The model's progressively optimistic – but also 'less likely' – scenarios indicate how vision should be translated into action. Population control, changes in lifestyle, and resource-saving and pollution-reducing technology would enable us to live within the planet's environmental limits. The question is, of course, if and how these general recommendations translate into concrete policy-making.

Combining the findings of a biodiversity index, the Living Planet Index, with the Ecological Footprint, the *Living Planet Report* (World Wide Fund for Nature *et al.* 2010: Chapter 3) gives a number of recommendations for a 'green economy'. The recommendations are more detailed than the above management rules, including:

- supplementing the report's indices with other indicators that could do what GDP cannot do, which is to measure well-being;
- investment in natural capital;

- protection of 'biomes' of forests, freshwater and oceans, setting aside at least 15 per cent of space to this end;
- equitable distribution of energy, food and other natural resources by allocating 'national budgets' for key resources;
- fostering local governance, international action and public–private cooperation.

If this sounds like the agenda of a United Nations conference, it is: the intention is to make the issues raised in the report the 'centrepiece' of the forthcoming Rio+20 summit (Chapter 10).

Rich-country organizations argued for dematerialization by **delinking** (or decoupling) **pollution and natural resource use from economic growth** (Organisation for Economic Co-operation and Development (OECD) 2002; Commission of the European Communities 2005; see Figure 4.1). Not to be left behind, the United Nations Environment Programme (UNEP 2011a: 30) has now joined the decoupling calls, suggesting a 'tough' reduction of annual resource use in industrialized countries by a 'factor of 3 to 5'. Recommendations of changing lifestyles and fostering environmentally sound technology aim to achieve at least a relative delinking, where material inputs still increase, but at a lower rate than that of economic growth.

Figure 4.1 Delinking natural resource use from economic growth – a tunnel vision? Is halving material flows into the economy compatible with doubling economic wealth? Will there be sustainability at the end of the tunnel? Sustainability of what: the environment, the economy or society?

The question is: how much dematerialization should we encourage or enforce, and over what period of time? Is it Daly's (1996, 2005) constant sustainable 'throughput' (material flow through the economy), or the reduction of material flows by a factor of 2 or even 10 (Factor 10 Club 1994)? Will sustainability of economic growth or 'development' (Chapter 9) be the result?

The European Union's natural resource strategy recognizes that lack of knowledge and data precludes setting quantitative targets (Commission of the European Communities 2005). Its strategy of relative decoupling is an indication that member states are not willing to abandon or slow down economic growth (cf. Chapter 10). Similarly, the OECD (2002: 5) admits that its 'decoupling concept lacks an automatic link to the environment's capacity to sustain, absorb or resist pressures of various kinds'. Consequently the strategy resorts to conventional environmental policy of monitoring compliance with international targets and recommending follow-up action. Even former followers now see the Factor 4 increase in resource productivity more as a 'directional guide' than a concrete policy prescription (Hinterberger *et al.* 2000; Bringezu 2002).

Suggestions for tackling ecological limits abound. To bring some order into proliferating sustainability targets and policy recommendations one can distinguish four **basic strategies** (Bartelmus 2008); they reflect different attitudes towards environmental limits in production and consumption:

- ignoring the limits and letting markets evaluate and deal with scarce environmental services;
- embracing limits, showing sufficiency in consumption and corporate social (and environmental) responsibility in production;
- pushing the limits for production through eco-efficiency;
- enforcing limits by rules and regulations for producers and consumers.

Mainstream economists tend to ignore environmental impacts as external to their models of supply and demand and economic growth. Environmental economists still prefer the invisible hand of **the market** to the rough elbow of regulation: budgeting for environmental costs allows market negotiation to determine the efficient use of environmental services (Chapters 5 and 7). Ecological economists may not shun market incentives and disincentives if they help changing lifestyles and production patterns. But they consider the marginal costing and pricing of such incentives as at best a supplementary tool. At worst, they see it as little more than 'puzzle solving' (Funtowicz and Ravetz 1991). Marginal adjustments of market behaviour cannot, in their view, deal with the severity of environmental effects on nature and people. What we need is a profound change of hearts and minds through vision, education and information (Meadows *et al.* 2004; Daly 2005; IUCN 2006).

A new environmental ethics* might bring about frugality in the consumption of goods and services. **Sufficiency** is the answer to greed and 'conspicuous consumption' (Veblen 1899/1967; Frank 1999). The rewards of a simpler 'good life' would be physical well-being and spiritual gratification from solidarity with the world's poor and future generations (Sachs 1995; Segal 1999). But who is to monitor and control overconsumption? Frugality and moderation have been preached since ancient times (Figure 4.2), without much success. Unfettered greed has indeed been the cause for the 2008–9 economic crisis. Still, do we really want governments, churches and activists to determine what is good for us?

Ecological economists seek to change corporate behaviour, too. They do this with tools of advocacy, suasion and information. Some enterprises do now tout **corporate social responsibility** for their environmental impacts on neighbourhoods and beyond (Figure 4.3). In this, they are encouraged by international organizations.* But should boardrooms become environmental and social policy-makers? In reality, caring about environmental stakeholders, at the possible expense of the company's shareholders, might work only in times of high profits or for purposes of corporate image building.

The Business Council for Sustainable Development, a predecessor of the World Business Council for Sustainable Development (WBCSD n.d.),

Figure 4.2 μηδέν ἄγαν, nothing in excess: supposedly an inscription on the ancient temple of Apollo at Delphi.

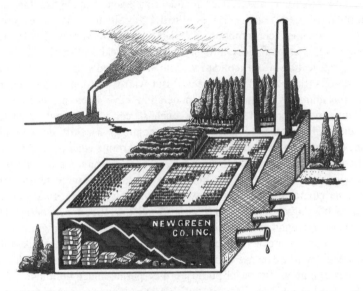

Figure 4.3 Corporate social responsibility. The *Newgreen* company cares now about the environment. Will lowering the flows of pollutants (and increasing costs) reduce revenues and profits?

which is a coalition of some 200 international companies, coined **eco-efficiency** as an effective environmental strategy of enterprises. Essentially, eco-efficiency is a matter of environmentally sound technology, which allows continuing or even increasing economic output with less environmental impact. Together with sufficiency it is the micro-economic counterpart of the macro-economic dematerialization strategy. Note that the Factor 4 goal of quadrupling resource productivity (Chapter 3) also puts its faith in examples of improved technologies, heralding an 'efficiency revolution' (von Weizsäcker *et al.* 1997: xviii).

A more ambitious version of eco-efficiency is metabolic consistency. Consistent production and consumption techniques are in harmony with nature's metabolism. Some even argue that such harmony results in zero emissions since nature supposedly does not generate any waste.* Most ecological economists do not see technology as the saviour, however, as it has been the culprit of many environmental sins (cf. Chapter 7). They also stress rebound effects from resource savings that could increase production, consumption and consequently environmental impacts. For example, the use of more fuel-efficient cars, which are less costly to drive, might increase driving and car purchases. Jevons (1865/1965) is credited with originally raising this issue for improved fuel production in the United Kingdom.

The least effective strategy is probably moral suasion, as in calls for changes to our lifestyles. It may pave the way, though, for accepting stronger measures of environmental rules and regulations. Imminent, irreversible and potentially catastrophic environmental impacts would justify such a proactive response. **Command and control** policies set and enforce environmental standards and regulations. Typical measures are the prohibition of hazardous products and production processes, the prescription of specific production techniques, including reuse and recycling of wastes, obligatory insurance for potential environmental damage and land appropriation for conservation. Command and control measures can ensure fast and transparent implementation, but need to be implemented in time to avoid the situation of Figure 4.4. The measures also need to survive the legislative period when they were enacted. Politics may well shorten the life of rules and regulations intended to address long-term sustainability issues. Remote bureaucracies that implement rules and regulations tend also to be less knowledgeable and efficient than *in situ* consumers and producers (cf. Chapter 7).

When it comes to **implementation**, the above strategies refer to a profusion of environmental protection measures. Environmental standards, regulations, fiscal incentives, education, information and advocacy reflect widely differing and frequently conflicting priorities and policies. The basic problem is the lack of a unifying framework or theory for ecological economics. Such a framework should facilitate the integrative analysis of how to sustain

Figure 4.4 Command and control. Legislation and rules prohibit environmentally damaging production and consumption practices such as slash and burn in deforestation. To be effective, rules and regulations need to be enforced by the executive powers. Such response to environmental destruction comes often too late or is abandoned too early.

the environment and economic activity. Existing measures and models of ecological economics fail to clearly link environmental limits and economic activities. They also fail to show what combinations of environmental and economic policies are most efficient in meeting environmental and economic objectives. Integration is indeed the key to sustainability. Part 2 explores economic theory and accounting to this end.

Want to know more?

The thresholds of ecosystem resilience are difficult to establish. Ciriacy-Wantrup (1952) and Bishop (1978) proposed, therefore, to set **safe minimum standards** (SMS) that extend conventional cost–benefit analysis to environmental concerns (Chapter 5). The purpose is to insure against uncertain, irreversible and unacceptable impacts. Crowards (1996) critically reviews the rather opaque notions of uncertainty, irreversibility and acceptability adopted for determining the SMS. Nonetheless, ecological economists picked up the idea of SMS for making the norms of ecological sustainability and sustainable development more operational (Chapter 9).

Contrary to relatively objective assessments of how much nature there is and will be (and, to some extent, we need), prescriptions of what we should do lead into the realm of morals and ethics. Ecological economists reject the utilitarian notion of *homo oeconomicus*, unworthy of *homo sapiens* (Faber *et al.* 2002). Continuing overexploitation of the planet's resources calls, in their view, for frugality and, where necessary, environmental regulation (Rennings *et al.* 1999). A new **environmental ethics** underlies these calls and their prescriptions. Environmental ethics goes beyond frugality, recognizing the 'intrinsic value' of nature and in particular of non-human life (Elliot 2001). Also, limits in the availability of nature's services raise issues of equity in their distribution, within and between generations. See Part 3 for the discussion of this social dimension of sustainable development. The difficulty of reaching consensus on philosophical questions is the reason why the Rio Earth Summit abandoned the idea of creating an Earth Charter in favour of a weaker, human-needs-oriented, Rio Declaration (United Nations 1994). Non-governmental organizations continue to promote an Earth Charter Initiative <http://www.earthcharter.org/> (accessed 19 June 2011).

Profit-maximizing enterprises are the institutional embodiment of *homo oeconomicus*. It may therefore be surprising that a growing number of enterprises seem to subscribe to **corporate social responsibility**, possibly in response to calls by international organizations (Crook 2005). The United Nations promote corporate social responsibility as part of public–private partnership (United Nations 2003) and of a Global Compact (United Nations Procurement Division 2004). The European Commission, Enterprise and Industry (2011) committed 'to promote Corporate Social Responsibility as a key element in ensuring long term employee and consumer trust'. It remains to be seen whether the recent economic downturn has thwarted corporate social responsibility. Corporate environmental accountants (Gray and Bebbington 2007) are sceptical: despite their sustainability rhetoric, corporations are bound to be accountable to shareholders rather than to environmental stakeholders.

The beauty of **metabolic consistency** (Huber 2004) or biomimicry (as it is sometimes called: Biomimicry Institute 2007–2011), is the idea of copying nature's production processes. The Zero Emissions Research and Initiative (2011) believes that fully reusing or recycling any waste and pollutants in production can change the mindsets that dominate markets; poverty alleviation and sustainability would be the result. However, the limited amount of – mostly agricultural – case studies has not so far been able to turn consistency into a silver bullet for greening the economy. Cradle-to-cradle design of production caters to similar objectives, but is probably overoptimistic in vying for the 'transformation' of cradle-to-grave economics (McDonough and Braungart 2003). Some industrial ecologists also contest the no-waste-in-nature argument (Ehrenfeld and Chertow 2002).

Points for discussion

- Do we need economics for either visionary changes of hearts and minds or rules for good environmental behaviour?
- How useful are calls for sufficiency in consumption, and corporate social responsibility in production? Are they heralds of a new environmental ethics?
- Command and control are effective instruments of policy implementation; they are also more judgemental. Who are or should be the judges?
- Is delinking environmental impacts from economic growth the main overall strategy of attaining ecological sustainability? How practical is it?
- What should be the purpose of a unifying framework or theory of ecological economics? Do we need it?

Part 2

Economic sustainability

How much for nature?

5 What is the value of nature?

- Environmentalists (and some ecological economists) accept *nature's own values* rather than economic ones
- Environmental economists recognize the *scarcity of environmental services*; they put a price on environmental externalities to correct market failure
- *Cost–benefit analysis* offers techniques *for* determining *economic values* of environmental goods and services
- *Discounting* future environmental costs and benefits obtains their net present value
- Estimates of the *cost of global warming* differ widely
- The *world's value of nature's services* might exceed world GDP

A cynic, according to Oscar Wilde, is 'a man who knows the price of everything and the value of nothing'. For environmentalists this could be the definition of an economist (Figure 5.1); but do *they* know the value of nature?

Material flow accounts show the economic system embedded in the physical world – a world that poses ultimate limits to the provision of economic and environmental goods and services. Ecological economists believe that we have violated these limits. Nature's own values of survival and reproduction should therefore overrule human preferences (Chapter 3). Disdaining economic pricing of nature, environmentalists and ecological economists resort to ethics or vision for setting environmental norms and standards (Chapter 4). Implementing the standards by rules and regulations does not leave much room for choice, the backbone of economic theory. Curbing population growth and economic activity appears to be the only way to save the earth.

Figure 5.1 The value of nature: do economists know it?

Environmental economists are more optimistic about our closeness to ultimate environmental limits. They consider the evidence for environmental disaster as inconclusive but admit to increasing **scarcity of environmental services**. In this case, we do have choices. We can pay for and use scarce economic and environmental goods and services according to their costs and our preferences. The problem is that despite their scarcity the necessary rationing tool, the market price, may not be available: nature's services are usually not, or not correctly, traded and valued in markets. Table 5.1 classifies environmental non-market effects as intended or unintended impacts by and on producers, consumers and the government.

Figure 5.2 depicts the classic example of a non-priced negative impact: smoke from a factory dirties the nearby laundry with impunity since markets ignore the damage of pollution. Economists call such unaccounted effects an externality. Externalities are unintended impacts of production and consumption on other production and consumption activities. **Environmental externalities** are, in particular, the effects of pollution and wastes on the production costs of producers and the health and well-being of consumers. Depletion of natural resources could be an externality if it is unintentional as in the case of the 'tragedy of the commons' (Chapter 3). Governmental mismanagement can also generate external effects if lack of knowledge or bureaucratic inefficiency is the cause. Conspicuous consumption (Chapter 4) can produce an external consumer–consumer effect: unnecessary

Table 5.1 Environmental non-market effects of economic activity and policy

Economic agents	Unintended externalities			Intended effects		
	Producers	Consumers	Government	Producers	Consumers	Government
Producers	Pollution, depletion	Pollution, ecological services		Illegal market control	Corporate social responsibility, recycling	Environmental lobbying, corruption
Consumers	Pollution	Pollution, conspicuous consumption			Recycling, reuse	Environmental lobbying, corruption
Government	Policy failure (errors, inefficiency)	Policy failure (errors, inefficiency)		Environmental regulation	Environmental protection	

and possibly unhealthy overconsumption could be the result of 'keeping up with the Joneses'. Environmental externalities can also be positive. Agriculture often creates pleasing landscapes and habitats for species, such as birds and hedgehogs, and may preserve genetic resources.

Intentional non-market effects in Table 5.1 can be beneficial or detrimental. Governments provide **public goods** such as security and environmental protection. Markets cannot or should not deal with such goods and services because their use does not affect supply, and nobody can or should be

Figure 5.2 Environmental externality: Pigou's (1920) smokestack-and-laundry example. Who bears the damage of pollution? Who should pay for it?

excluded from their benefits. Comparatively inefficient government, rather than the market, has to decide, therefore, on the provision of public goods to society. The question is, how much of a good thing do we need? In the absence of markets, cost–benefit analysis helps to evaluate governmental programmes and projects (Chapter 7). Socially responsible corporations (Chapter 4) and individuals may also create positive non-market effects on purpose. They could protect or improve environmental conditions in their neighbourhood, and reuse or recycle their wastes. On the other hand, an 'uncivil' society of consumers and producers can generate *public 'bads'*. Table 5.1 shows corruption and non-criminal but still distortive lobbying as the intended manipulation of government policy by producers and consumers. Powerful oil and coal mining companies are known, for example, to pressure governments into subsidizing production at the expense of the environment.

Ignoring environmental externalities is an important reason for **market failure**. Markets fail because they cannot find and apportion the correct scarcity values of externalities to economic activities. Basic textbook economics tells us that ignoring these effects by those responsible for them causes the misallocation of scarce resources. As a result, the economy generates less economic welfare than it could if economic agents bore the costs of inflicting environmental damage and reap the benefits of free services.* For this reason, environmental economists propose the use of market instruments for 'internalizing' externalities into the plans and budgets of economic agents (Chapter 7).

Different **valuation techniques**, including those used in cost–benefit analysis, can assess scarcity values. Depending on the effects of environmental externalities on consumers or producers, one can distinguish:

- demand-side valuations, which try to measure people's well-being gained (utility) or lost (damage) from a decrease or an increase of environmental impacts; and
- supply-side valuations, which measure the costs of using environmental services in production and of mitigating environmental impacts, notably by the government.

Demand-side valuations include interviews, simulation of markets, estimates of travel cost to environmental amenities, and comparisons of real estate with different environmental qualities. In particular, surveys of the willingness to pay for the use of environmental amenities, or to be compensated for their loss, seek to assess the utility or damage value of environmental services. Demand-side valuations are controversial. They suffer from well-known problems of measuring and aggregating utility, which includes hardly quantifiable 'consumer surplus'.* Further distortions include free-rider attitudes and ignorance about environmental effects in interviews (Figure 5.3). Supply-side valuations of costing the avoidance or reduction of environmental impacts are less controversial. They are well established in cost-effectiveness analyses* and can build on the accounting tools of enterprises and national environmental accounts (Chapter 6).

Figure 5.4 shows the different categories of the **total economic value** of an environmental amenity. Economists define the total value of an environmental asset like a forest or beach as the utility or welfare derived from the actual use, optional use or non-use of the asset. Non-use can be a source of well-being when it creates satisfaction about the conservation of nature and its species. Ultimately, the idea is to combine supply and demand in fictitious (modelled) markets for environmental services. Under ideal competitive market conditions the resulting prices determine the optimal use value of environmental goods and services.*

Figure 5.3 How much for an elephant? Willingness-to-pay surveys suffer from ignorance about the costs and benefits of maintaining environmental amenities and free-rider attitudes of respondents. Who should put a value on our 'life companions'? Does it make sense to add up the above values?

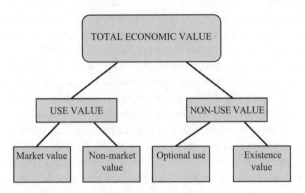

Figure 5.4 The total economic value of an environmental amenity consists mostly
of welfare generated by actual use, e.g. of fish caught and sold or non-
marketed recreation found in nature. Optional use and non-use may also
create welfare through satisfaction about reserving natural resources for
future generations or from knowledge about the existence of cherished
species such as elephants or dolphins.

To assess the long-term sustainability of the supply and use of economic and environmental goods and services, one would have to find
their expected costs and benefits. Ecological economists tend to treat this
question as a matter of ethics (Chapter 4). Solidarity with future generations demands that we leave them an intact environment. This may reflect
nature's own values, but it is still a human judgement by those who hold
nature in particularly high esteem. Should their opinion and high standards
overrule economic preferences that consider future and uncertain costs and
benefits as less significant than current ones?

Economists answer in the negative. They point out that markets **discount**
the investment in a durable capital good to a lower present value since the
returns to this investment are not earned immediately but in the future.
Despite the absence of markets for environmental assets, environmental
economists and accountants extend this discounting to the value of 'natural
capital' (Chapters 6 and 7). Discounting future environmental damage to its
present value is rather optimistic when reserving lower funds now to tackle
damage in the future. Note that funds 'freed' in this way can earn interest or
returns from other investments.

Applying a lower social discount rate reflects the pessimistic environmentalist view of pending disaster. Zero discounting, in particular, treats future
damage as if it were to happen any moment. This would require budgeting
the full cost now of preventing or mitigating the potential damage. Inter-
generational equity reinforces this argument. Adding future damage costs

to present ones assumes that the current generation feels the pain of future generations as much as its own. Figure 5.5 applies discount rates to the case of the 'worst possible nuclear accident'. Such an assessment would burden the current population of a country with the enormous total damage costs of up to US$8 trillion. Marginal economic analysis becomes irrelevant in this case. On the other hand, the figure shows that discounting future damage saves economic analysis from irrelevance: even low discount rates reduce dramatically the present value of environmental damage and its mitigation costs.

Climate change is a good example to illustrate the effects of discounting and welfare valuation, and their validity. Chapter 2 described global warming as a surrogate for environmental deterioration. It also pointed out that only a comparison with other environmental and socio-economic concerns could assess the relative significance of global warming. In the absence of a common physical measuring rod, our best bet is to use economic values to make this comparison. Table 5.2 illustrates with a few key examples the wide range of **global cost estimates for climate change**. The costs are either damage from inaction, or abatement costs from responsive action.

The widely discussed review by Stern (2006) warns that inaction might generate a global warming of 5–6°C by the year 2100. Such

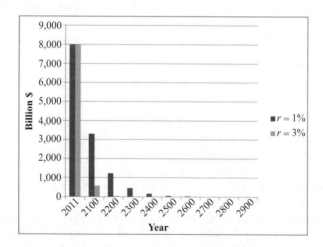

Figure 5.5 Discounting the damage of a nuclear meltdown. The damage from the worst possible outcome of a nuclear accident may be as high as US$8 trillion (Welfens 2012). Applying a relatively low discount rate of 1 per cent lowers the present value of the damage and corresponding investment in mitigation to less than half, assuming that the accident will happen by the end of the century. A higher, frequently applied rate of 3 per cent obtains only 7 per cent of the original value. Expecting the accident after 500 years discounts the anticipated damage to negligible values even for the low discount rate.

Table 5.2 Global cost of climate change

	Total damage costs ($, % of GDP)	Total abatement costs ($, % of GDP)	Net gain ($, % of GDP)
IPCC (2007b)	1–5%[a]	0.2–2.5%[b]	
Stern (2006)	5–20%[c] $2.5–9.8 trillion[d]	1% (–2% to 5%)[e]	$2.5 trillion[f] 0.13%[g]
Nordhaus (2008)	$22.6 trillion[h] 2.5%[i]	$2.2 trillion[j]	$3.1 trillion[k] 0.16%[l]

Notes:
a   Global mean loss for 4°C global warming by mid- to end-century.
b   In 2030, for stabilizing greenhouse gas concentration in the atmosphere in 2100 or later at 535–590 ppm CO_2 equivalents (CO_2-eq), resulting in global temperature increase of 2.8–3.2°C over pre-industrial levels; costs are percentages of baseline GDP.
c   Average loss of welfare (percentage of global per-capita consumption 'now and forever'), assuming 5–6°C global warming by 2100.
d   In 2006.
e   In 2050, annual cost of 500–550 ppm CO_2-eq stabilization.
f   Net present (2006) value of benefits of strong action now (zero time preference discounting).
g   Percentage of total future discounted world income, estimated at $2,000 trillion by Nordhaus (2008).
h   Present value (2005, discount rate 4%) for no-emission control and global warming of 3.1°C (since 1900 and by 2100).
i   'Best guess' for 2100.
j   Present value of optimal policy at $7.4 carbon (dioxide) tax in 2005, increasing to $55.1 in 2100.
k $5.3 trillion (damage reduction: not shown in the table) minus $2.2 trillion (abatement cost), limiting global warming to 2.6°C in 2100.
l   Percentage of discounted total future income ($2,000 trillion).

temperature increase would bring about damages of at least 5 per cent of global per-capita consumption 'now and forever' (Stern 2006: x). On the other hand, spending about 1 per cent of the world's GDP by 2050 would stabilize greenhouse gas concentrations and keep global warming below 3°C. Strong action now would gain us a high net present benefit of 2.5 trillion US dollars (discounted at rather obscure rates).

This gain appears to be similar to the US$3 trillion of net present benefits calculated by Nordhaus's (2008) model of optimal climate policy. The benefits are the result of applying an optimal carbon price (and tax) to the world economy (Chapter 7). Nordhaus (2008: 87) dismisses, however, Stern's modelling as 'extremely expensive'. In a special model run he applies Stern's 'near-zero' discounting to climate investments while applying more realistic real interest rates of about 5.5 per cent to the rest of the economy. A loss of US$14 trillion, rather than any gain, appears to be the outcome of Stern's high and costly early emission reduction. Stern justifies his low discounting as a matter of inter-generational equity, which discredits any significant discounting.

The extensive footnotes of Table 5.2 indicate that all cost and benefit figures are at best rough estimates. This is the case despite the reliance of both Stern and Nordhaus on generally accepted physical and monetary data provided by the Intergovernmental Panel on Climate Change (IPCC 2007a, 2007b). Different concepts, time frames, coverage of climate impacts, valuations, modelling techniques and model assumptions impair the comparability of these and many other cost calculations (see also Chapter 7). The inconvenient truth is: we do not have an unequivocal evaluation of the importance of climate change.

A group of ecological economists defied the problems of global welfare measurement and assessed the **value of the world's ecosystem services** (Costanza *et al.* 1997b). Their estimate of US$33 trillion in 1994 exceeds that year's value of GDP by US$6 trillion (Figure 5.6). The world's people thus appear to be willing to spend more on nature than they earn – a highly improbable suggestion. Apart from the difficulty of covering the myriad of ecosystems and their services, the study takes on the non-measurable, marginal utility and global welfare.

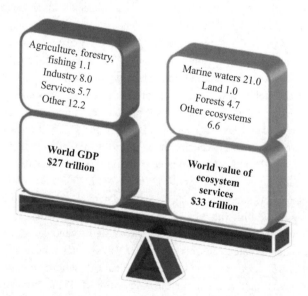

Figure 5.6 How much for nature? How much for economic output? Costanza *et al.* (1997b) estimated the value of the world's ecosystem services in 1994 at US$33 trillion within a confidence range of US$16 to US$54 trillion. World GDP then was US$26.9 trillion at current prices.

If nothing else, the bewildering array of monetary values for climate change effects and nature's services indicates that there *are* environmental costs to be reckoned with. Conventional economic analysis and policy ignores (externalizes) these costs. For a more accurate picture of economic performance, the costs of environmental depletion and degradation need to be accounted for – preferably in a commonly agreed system or framework. Such a framework should provide clear concepts, compatible environmental and economic classifications, and commensurable indicators. The next chapter endeavours to do just this by expanding the widely used economic accounts and balance sheets.

Want to know more?

Market failure from externalities is basic textbook economics. Together with other external effects, environmental externalities prevent the attainment of maximum welfare, referred to in economic analysis as **Pareto optimality**. In a Pareto-optimal situation, generated under perfectly competitive conditions, no change in production and consumption patterns can improve the well-being of any person without detracting from the well-being of another person. The reason is that in competitive markets the prices of goods and services are equal to their marginal production cost and consumption utility. At this point, the economy is in a state of general equilibrium. The economic welfare generated by Pareto optimality ignores distributional effects such as welfare gains from poverty alleviation. This is a social concern, addressed in particular by the sustainable development paradigm (Chapter 9). For the analysis of long-term sustainability economists suggested to aim at 'potential Pareto improvement' for 'dynamic efficiency'; the inter-generational distribution of welfare should be left to politics (Stavins *et al.* 2003).

Demand and supply in actual or modelled markets determine the price as the **optimal unit value** of the most efficient uses of natural resources and environmental sinks. Figure 5.7 shows the demand curve D for an environmental source or sink service (ES) as a function of marginal benefit (MB) from using the service. The value of marginal benefits (and willingness to pay) could increase towards infinity with mounting scarcity of vital resources such as water, air or fertile land. The supply curve S represents the marginal costs (MC) of supplying the environmental service. The near-vertical part of the supply curve shows limited availability of the service, obtained from an exhaustible natural asset. In this case, the marginal supply costs tend to become infinite as supply approaches its limit. The supply and demand curves intersect at point I, where actual or simulated supply and demand negotiate a consensus price p. In turn, price p determines the optimal use level es_{opt} of the environmental service. The figure also shows the sub-optimal oversupply $\overline{es}$ that could occur when cost-effectiveness analysis replaces the marginal benefits curve D by a fixed standard $\overline{D}$ of maximum use of the environmental service.

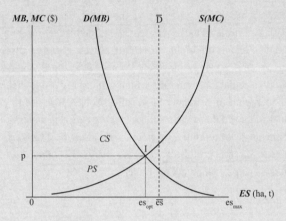

Figure 5.7 Economic values of an environmental service.

Figure 5.7 illustrates the different **economic values** that determine the costs and benefits of environmental services:

- The product of es_{opt} and p is the actual (observed) or hypothetical (estimated or modelled) **market value** of the environmental service.
- If we add the – most likely indeterminate (no intersection of D and the ordinate) – consumer surplus *CS* (under the demand curve D and above the $\overline{pI}$ line) to the market value, we obtain the equally indeterminate **total economic** (welfare) **value** of the environmental service (for an overview, see Dziegielewska 2009). This is because *CS* reflects the willingness of consumers to pay a higher price than p for each amount of the service that is lower than es_{opt}. Note that the total economic value can only be determined for environmental services, for which close-to-zero supply at a limited cost level would be acceptable to consumers, at a reasonable price.
- In case of non-priced, non-marketed (free) goods and services CS actually represents their total economic value.

- Producer surplus *PS* (above the supply curve, up to the market price line $\overline{p1}$) or **rent** of a priced resource is the **net value to the supplier** of a natural resource or service; considering that the supply curve represents the marginal cost of supply, this value is the producer's short-term profit (ignoring fixed costs) from selling an environmental resource or service.

Over the lifetime of the resource the discounted value of all the net benefits (rents) gained is an estimate of the **value of the natural capital** stock, from which environmental services are drawn (cf. Chapter 6). It is at this value that an environmental asset would be traded if there were a market for it. Such estimates are highly uncertain, however, as new discoveries, notably of oil and gas deposits, affect resource prices. Beyond economic profitability, a social discount rate, which is normally lower than the rate of return to capital investment, could reflect society's desire to preserve a natural asset for future generations. Hepburn (2007) reviews the use of discount rates for attaining economic efficiency or inter-generational equity; declining rates might 'reduce the tension' (Hepburn 2007: 120) between the two philosophical positions.

Points for discussion

- Why do markets ignore environmental problems? Should they deal with all environmental source and sink services and the natural assets that provide them?
- Should we have a market for environmental protection?
- Is pricing the priceless an oxymoron? How can we measure the source and sink services of nature and compare them with economic goods and services? Why should we do so?
- What is the value of an elephant (Figure 5.3)?
- What are the costs of action and inaction on climate change (Table 5.1)? Is it a good idea to discount uncertain but possibly disastrous future effects of climate change?
- What is the economic value of nature (Figure 5.8)? Do we need to know?
- What are the costs of climate change? Do we need to know them?
- Is adding up the weight (mass) of material inputs a better way of assessing the significance of the environment for our well-being and the sustainability of economic activity?

6   Accounting for economic sustainability

- Economic sustainability can be defined in theory as *non-declining economic welfare*
- The *Genuine Progress Indicator* is a flawed measure of economic welfare
- The *System for integrated Environmental and Economic Accounting* introduces natural capital into the System of National Accounts
- Produced and natural *capital maintenance* is an operational concept of economic sustainability
- Maintaining the value of produced and natural capital obtains *weak sustainability*
- Positive environmentally adjusted net capital formation indicates a *sustainable world economy*
- *Negative capital formation* of African and Latin American countries *signals non-sustainability* of their economies

The valuation techniques of Chapter 5 help assess the economic significance of environmental assets and their services. Their values do not tell us, however, whether they are sustainable or how they affect the sustainability of the economy. With the objective of welfare maximization in mind, economists define **economic sustainability** as non-declining economic welfare (Pezzey 1989). In practice, GDP or personal consumption serves as a proxy welfare measure, despite national accountants arguing 'against the welfare interpretations of the accounts' and their indicators (European Commission *et al.* 2009: 12). Still, GDP continues to be blamed for misrepresenting the economic welfare and happiness of society.*

Economists Nordhaus and Tobin (1973) attempted to turn net national product into a more convincing **measure of economic welfare**. They added the value of welfare-enhancing household services and leisure, and deducted the value of externalities and 'regrettable' expenditures. Further costing (deduction of the value) of a 'capital-widening requirement' (Nordhaus and Tobin 1973: 514) is to sustain per-capita consumption of a growing population. Regrettables also go under the name of defensive expenditures, which are thought to maintain rather than increase human welfare; they include environmental protection and other costs of mitigating the hazards of transportation, disease and security (Leipert 1989).

Some ecological economists realized that their ecological sustainability concept (Chapter 3) lacks a connection with economic activity. They took up the idea of correcting personal consumption for purposes of welfare measurement and advanced an **Indicator of Sustainable Economic Welfare** (ISEW). Unsurprisingly, the ISEW leans heavily toward the negative side of welfare losses (Daly and Cobb 1989). The intention is apparently to prove a 'threshold hypothesis' (Max-Neef 1995), according to which welfare reaches a turning point because of the effects of high-level economic growth. First estimates of a modified ISEW, the Genuine Progress Indicator (GPI), seemed to confirm the hypothesis for the USA (Cobb *et al.* 1995). Revised calculations, shown in Figure 6.1, dilute the hypothesis: they indicate stagnating welfare since the 1970s, with GDP continuing to increase (at least until the 2008–9 recession).

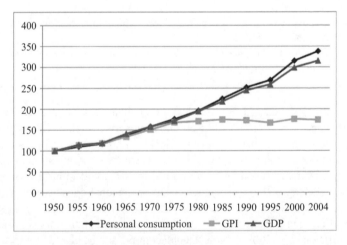

Figure 6.1 GPI, GDP and personal consumption per capita, USA, 1950–2004 (in constant prices, 1950 = 100). GDP and personal consumption moved in tandem with the GPI until the 1970s. Since then they have separated in a scissor movement: economic welfare (GPI) has stagnated while the economy has shown steady growth (until 2004).

Source: Talberth *et al.* (2007).

Major flaws impair the validity of the GPI as a measure of sustainable welfare. They include:

- the arbitrary selection and distinction of regrettable and desirable expenditures. Should we really count expenses for environmental protection, natural disasters, defence, security and accidents as regrettables when in most cases we would be worse off without them? How about food and drinks with detrimental health effects?
- the opaque valuation mix of market values for natural resource use with controversial welfare/damage values for ecosystem services and environmental externalities;
- the mixing of non-comparable and possibly overlapping sustainability concepts of non-declining welfare and capital maintenance.

The merit of the GPI is to draw attention to the misuse of GDP as a welfare measure. The authors seem to be blinded, though, by their antagonism towards mainstream economics, proclaiming that the GPI 'would blast away the obfuscatory polemics of growth – and the devious politics that goes with it' (Cobb *et al.* 1995: 72). Unfortunately they throw out the baby with the bath water, ignoring possibilities of using the quantifiable concepts and checks and balances of the national accounts for modifying economic indicators.

The United Nations **System for integrated Environmental and Economic Accounting** (SEEA) applies as much as possible the conventions of the System of National Accounts (SNA) adopted world-wide.* The fundamental approach of the SEEA is to define, classify and introduce natural capital in the national accounts. Figure 6.2 illustrates the inclusion of 'environmental assets' (an accounting term for natural capital) in stock (asset) and flow (supply and use) accounts. The shaded areas represent the environmental part of the integrated accounts. The figure also shows the overlap of the two types of accounts, where changes in stocks are flows of capital formation and capital consumption. The SEEA focuses on the measurable aspects of sustainability, which are the costs of avoiding a decline in income, output and environmental assets, rather than the welfare effects of such decline. For this, the SEEA argues for the use of market prices for natural resources that are traded in markets, and of maintenance costs for avoiding or reducing environmental externalities.

As a result of the incorporation of natural capital, the production accounts include not only the use and consumption of produced capital, but also the environmental cost of natural capital consumption. Natural capital consumption is the 'permanent' depletion and degradation of environmental assets – beyond natural regeneration. Corporate and

	PRODUCTION (i=1,2,...,n industries)	FINAL CONSUMPTION	CHANGES IN CAPITAL STOCKS	CHANGES IN CAPITAL STOCKS	REST OF THE WORLD
OPENING STOCKS			Produced assets	Environmental assets	
			+		
SUPPLY OF PRODUCTS	Outputs (O_i)				Imports (M)
USE OF PRODUCTS	Inputs (I_i)	Final consumption (C)	Gross capital formation (GCF)		Exports (X)
PRODUCED CAPITAL USE	Capital consumption (CC_p)		Capital consumption (CC_p)		
NATURAL CAPITAL USE	Environmental cost (EC) (of natural capital consumption)			Numerical capital consumption (CC_n)	
			+		
			Other asset changes	Other asset changes	
			=		
CLOSING STOCKS			Produced assets	Environmental assets	

Figure 6.2 SEEA: incorporating natural capital in the national accounts. The vertical asset accounts show the inclusion of natural capital (environmental assets) in opening and closing stocks at the beginning and end of an accounting period. During this period the changes in the value of natural and produced capital overlap with the flow (supply and use) accounts as capital formation and capital consumption. Note that the environmental costs of the production accounts are mirrored in the natural capital consumption value of the asset accounts, in line with the treatment of produced capital consumption in the conventional accounts. Other asset changes such as natural growth (in the wilderness) or the effects of natural disasters are not the result of economic activity; they are therefore excluded from the (costing and pricing of the) supply and use accounts.

Source: © Eolss Publishers Co Ltd. From Bartelmus (2001), modified, with permission from Eolss Publishers Co. Ltd.

national accountants practise sustainability when setting aside an allowance for replacing worn-out capital goods such as buildings or machines. They do this to prevent a decline in outputs and incomes. Such 'prudent conduct' (Hicks 1939: 172) is actually built into the key economic concept of income, which counts only net revenues that are sustained by saving and reinvestment.

Economists distinguish produced (fixed) capital from natural, human (labour) and social (networks) capital. Accounting for human and social capital is still quite undeveloped because of conceptual – what is capital consumption? – and measurement problems.* Considerable progress has been made, though, in natural capital accounting. This is one reason why this book focuses on sustainability issues that are brought about by the interaction of the environment and economy. It does not imply that 'non-countables' such as goodwill of businesses, trust or ethics do not count in sustaining the economy – they just do not add up (cf. Chapter 11).

It is a small logical and 'prudent' step to extend the concepts of capital consumption and maintenance from produced to natural capital. Making an allowance for reinvestment in and hence **maintenance of produced and natural capital** is **an operational concept of economic sustainability**. More specifically, it represents combined economic–environmental sustainability of production at the micro level, and of economic performance and growth at the macro level. The environmental part of this sustainability concept seeks to avoid a potential decrease in production and consumption because of the loss of exhaustible raw materials and the costs of environmental degradation. The necessary maintenance costs are a measure of how much society could and should have expended to avoid or mitigate environmental degradation and depletion. Investment in the maintenance of natural capital is an indicator of our caring about environmental quality and nature's contribution to prosperity now and in the future.

Deducting the cost allowances for produced and natural capital consumption from economic indicators obtains **environmentally adjusted net domestic product** (EDP) and **environmentally adjusted net capital formation** (ECF).* Note that EDP defines a green *net* domestic product, rather than the generally advocated green *gross* domestic product (GDP). Accounting only for natural capital consumption, but ignoring the consumption of produced capital by a green GDP, does not make much sense. The reason is that both produced and natural capital need to be maintained to sustain economic performance and growth. Crumbling infrastructure in the USA and many developing countries reminds us of the consequences of neglecting the wear and tear of capital goods.

Growing or at least non-declining EDP would indicate that the economy performed sustainably in the past. This is, however, just a starting point for assessing future performance. For predictions of future sustainability, one would have to model trends of EDP with the usual uncertainties and assumptions in projections of economic growth and its environmental impacts (Chapters 3 and 7). Lacking long time series of EDP, an alternative way of looking at economic sustainability is the use of ECF. Positive ECF indicates that investment in produced and natural capital increased the net value of capital. The economy performed sustainably in this case by keeping intact or even increasing the value of its productive capital base.

Maintaining the overall value of capital, rather than its physical stock, reflects **weak sustainability**. If reinvestment in a particular type of natural capital is not possible, other income-generating investments should take up the slack. Weak sustainability thus assumes that other production factors can, if necessary, replace the capital goods used up in production and income generation. Produced capital goods, in particular, should substitute for natural (non-produced and exhaustible) capital, at least at the level of actual use – and not in total as sometimes argued. As discussed in Chapter 3, weak sustainability thus ignores the existence of possibly irreplaceable 'critical' natural capital. Note also that ignoring human and social capital and its consumption – difficult to define and measure as they are – paints a limited picture of making our economies just 'more' sustainable.

Research institutes and national statistical services have carried out **case studies** of green accounting (Uno and Bartelmus 1998). Data users and producers are, however, reluctant to adopt the SEEA. In the USA, the coal-mining lobby, fearing disclosure of environmental impacts, succeeded in blocking further work by the Bureau of Economic Analysis (Landefeld and Howell 1998). Despite a positive review by a National Academy of Sciences panel (Nordhaus and Kokkelenberg 1999), green accounting is still on ice. Even the United Nations *et al.* (2003) delayed the publication of a revised 2003 version of the SEEA until now, when it adopted a reduced version as a 'statistical standard'.* Fear of competition and the costs of more comprehensive environmental-economic accounting might be behind the reluctance of official statisticians to modify their established accounts, even as a separate 'satellite' system.

Table 6.1 shows the results of a low-cost study of the German economy. Environmental maintenance costs ($EC = CC_n$) of 59 billion Deutschmarks are significant, amounting to 3 per cent of net domestic product. From a policy-making point of view, however, this is hardly an insurmountable problem for a rich country. Note that the wear and tear of produced capital (CC_p) is five times the environmental cost, indicating that the usual focus on gross indicators such as GDP and GCF could be misleading when assessing the success or failure of economic policy. Another study by the author (Bartelmus 2009) estimated the environmental cost in the USA at that time at 1.6 per cent of net domestic product, increasing to 2.7 per cent in 2006.

Globally, environmental depletion and degradation costs amounted to about US$3 trillion or 6 per cent of world GDP in 2006 (Bartelmus 2009). During the relatively short time period of 1990–2006, the world economy showed similar growth rates for GDP and EDP. As mentioned, ECF paints a better and different picture of the potential sustainability of economic activity: it indicates the capacity to produce new capital after accounting for the wear and tear of produced capital and the destruction or degradation of natural capital. Figure 6.3 reveals large differences in the economic sustainability of economic growth for the world's major regions and countries. Positive ECF in industrialized countries and China shows sustainable economic growth. Negative ECF in developing countries, notably in Africa, indicates that these countries have been living off their natural and produced capital base. Overall,

Table 6.1 SEEA case study, Germany, 1990 (billion Deutschmarks)[a]

	Production	Final consumption	Changes in produced assets	Changes in environmental assets	Rest of the world
Output	$O = 6{,}007$				
Input	$I = 3{,}761$				
Final use	$GDP = O - I = C + GCF + X - M = 2{,}246$	$C = 1{,}610$	$GCF = 519$		$X - M = 117$
Produced capital use	$CC_p = 303$		$CC_p = 303$		
Net product	$NDP = GDP - CC_p = 1{,}943$		$NCF = GCF - CC_p = 216$		
Natural capital use	$EC = 59$			$CC_n = 59$	
Greened net product	$EDP = NDP - EC = 1{,}884$		$ECF = NCF - EC = 157$		

Source: Bartelmus (2002), from Table II.3, with kind permission from Springer Science+Business Media B.V.

Note:

a See Figure 6.2 and end-of-chapter 'Want to know more?' section for an explanation of symbols and acronyms. Environmental costs and modified indicators are shown in the shaded cells.

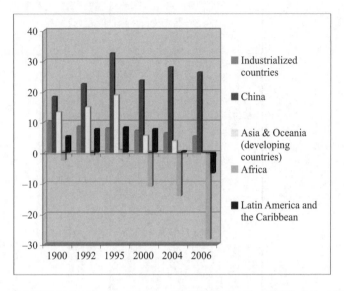

Figure 6.3 ECF in world regions (per cent of EDP). Positive ECF in industrialized countries and China indicates (weakly) sustainable economic growth. Negative ECF of developing countries of Africa and Latin America presents a non-sustainable economic performance that diminishes capital for consumption purposes. GDP growth in these countries presents a misleading picture of the sustainability of economic growth and development.

Source: Bartelmus (2009).

the world economy appears to be sustainable, at least in terms of economic sustainability. This is quite different from what environmentalists tell us about ecological non-sustainability of a full world. Of course, weak economic and stronger ecological sustainability are not directly comparable (Chapter 3). In Chapter 8, we will look for some ways to overcome the discrepancy between assessments of ecological and economic sustainability.

This first compilation of global SEEA indicators relied on readily available international databases for environmental impacts and their costs. Data gaps, in particular for pollutants, are likely to cause considerable undercoverage. This could be one reason for the above-mentioned discrepancy of sustainability measures. Moreover, a number of methodological issues are still controversially debated. They include:

- the valuation of environmental degradation, which has been a sore point between national accountants and environmental economists, notably in the revision of the SEEA;*

- the aggregation of environmental impacts in physical (non-monetary) accounts, implying that physical data can reflect overall environmental damage (Chapter 2);
- the identification, measurement and (e)valuation of critical natural capital (Chapter 3);
- accounting for a broader sustainability concept, which includes the maintenance of human, social and institutional capital, possibly as part of the all-encompassing paradigm of sustainable development (Chapter 9);
- the inclusion of ecosystems and their services;
- transboundary flows of unsolicited wastes and pollutants;
- the links of national and corporate environmental accounts for improving data availability and quality, and comparing the environmental performance of economic agents with sectoral and national results.*

Want to know more?

GDP bashing has proliferated. Cobb *et al*. (1995) famously asked: 'If the GDP is up, why is America down?' Recently, Stiglitz *et al*. (2010) explained 'Why the GDP doesn't add up'; a European Union sponsored conference looked 'Beyond GDP' (European Commission 2007–10); and a one-day strategy session of American scholars and officials explored ways to 'dethrone GDP' (Talberth 2010). Also, do not miss Alan AtKisson's GDP song <http://www.youtube.com/watch?v=qxmVJnwWeTY> (accessed on 9 July 2011).

In 2008 the government of Bhutan adopted **gross national happiness** (GNH) as the measure on which the country's economic, cultural, environmental and spiritual policy should be based (Centre for Bhutan Studies 2008). Like other cornucopian concepts such as sustainable development (Chapter 9) or quality of life (Max-Neef 1995), the GNH is a broad measure of human well-being or welfare. Slightly less than half of Americans experience 'happiness or enjoyment without a lot of stress or worry' according to Gallup (2010) surveys. A World Data Base of Happiness seeks to synthesize research and surveys of happiness in people and nations <http://worlddatabaseofhappiness.eur.nl/> (accessed on 19 June 2011). National happiness seems to have become a rallying call for those looking for an alternative to GDP.

Almost all countries adopted the **System of National Accounts** (SNA) (European Commission *et al.* 2009) for the compilation of economic indicators. The indicators summarize activities of economic agents (government, households, enterprises, financial institutions, non-profit organizations). Accounting equations make up the system and define the indicators of economic performance. The most popular indicators are gross domestic product (GDP), net domestic product (NDP), outputs (O_i) and inputs (I_i) of a country's i = 1, 2, ..., n industries, as well as GDP components of final consumption of households (C), gross capital formation (GCF), produced capital consumption (CC_p), imports (M) and exports (X).

Some countries prefer to use gross national income (GNI) as the main indicator of overall economic performance. GNI differs from GDP by the amount of income payments and receipts to and from non-residents. The sustainability of an equitable distribution and use of income is more of a social concern addressed by the broad sustainable development paradigm (Chapter 9).

Bartelmus *et al.* (1991) developed the original **System for integrated Environmental and Economic Accounting** (SEEA). The SEEA (United Nations 1993) modifies the above accounting indicators, introducing the consumption of natural capital (CC_n) as environmental cost (EC) into the production accounts and balance sheets of the SNA (Figure 6.2). The greening of the economic indicators is the result of deducting the costs of natural capital consumption from net domestic product (NDP) and net capital formation. The following equations show how this turns GDP and gross capital formation (GCF) into environmentally adjusted indicators of EDP and ECF:

1 $\quad \sum O_i - \sum I_i = \text{GDP}$
2 $\quad \text{GDP} - CC_p = \text{NDP}$
3 $\quad \text{NDP} - \text{EC} = \text{EDP} = C + (\text{GCF} - CC_p - CC_n) + X - M$
4 $\quad \text{ECF} = \text{GCF} - CC_p - CC_n$

Much of the critique of the SEEA is about its valuations of non-market goods and services. Bartelmus (2001) discusses the pros and cons of 'pricing the priceless'. The latest **2012** version of the **SEEA** (Committee of Exports on Environmental Economic Accounting 2012) is sceptical about monetary valuation – except for the depletion of natural (economic) resources that enter markets. The 2012 SEEA relegates the assessment of environmental degradation to planned volumes or 'experimental ecosystem accounts' and 'extensions and applications'. Omitting environmental degradation from its 'central framework' makes it look like environmental-economic accounting without the environment. The result is a guidebook that is, at least in part, more a framework for environmental and economic data than a truly integrated environmental-economic accounting system.

Attempts at accounting for **human capital** treat expenditures for education, training and health as capital formation. For instance, the World Bank (2006) includes expenditure on education as capital investment in its adjusted net savings indicator. However, this includes educational services, which generate immediate satisfaction and are more in the nature of consumption than long-term investment; also, it is hardly possible to account for human capital 'depreciation' due to loss of knowledge and decreasing health. To quantify **social capital** is even more difficult because of non-marketed 'intangibles' such as networking, norms, social cohesion, trust and (sometimes also included) institutional and cultural capital. Recent handbooks on social capital therefore deal mostly with conceptual questions (Castiglione *et al.* 2008; Svendsen and Svendsen 2009).

In many ways **corporate environmental accounting** resembles the greening of the national accounts. The accountancy profession has been reluctant to embark on 'full-cost' accounting (including the cost of environmental externalities), favouring physical eco-balances and life cycle analysis of products (Bartelmus and Seifert 2003: Introduction). Two international guidelines of corporate environmental management include internal and external audits for the environmental performance of a corporation: the ISO 14000 standards (International Organization for Standardization 2011) are less stringent than the Environmental Management and Audit Scheme (EMAS) of the European Union (European Commission, Environment 2011). Application of the guidelines is voluntary; it is typically motivated by cost savings in natural resource use, compliance with actual or anticipated environmental rules and regulations, and an improved corporate image of environmental accountability.

Points for discussion

- What should we sustain: nature, welfare, happiness, development, income or economic growth? What is measurable and manageable?
- GDP bashing is fashionable. Are welfare and happiness indicators better measures?
- Should one deduct defensive expenditures from GDP? Should we remove all outputs of industries that produce inputs into the production of regrettables? What would be left of the economy?
- Do the modified indicators of the SEEA measure sustainability? Does the SEEA succeed in pricing the priceless?
- Why do environmentalists, economists and statistical offices tend to ignore the SEEA?
- Is weak sustainability of capital maintenance a useful feature of economic performance? Why not use strong sustainability (Chapter 3)?
- Why do most corporations still ignore environmental (full-cost) accounting? What would environmental costing do to their bottom line?
- What do you make of the – hitherto unaccounted for – environmental costs of 2–3 per cent of GDP in the USA and about 13 per cent in China? As we asked in Chapter 1: do (the costs of) environmental problems outweigh economic benefits?
- What is measurable is manageable! Do you agree? Can we ignore intangible assets and their services, notably of human and social capital?

7 What should we do about it?

- Environmental externalities and inefficiencies in the provision of public goods are responsible for *market failures*
- *Cost–benefit analysis* helps governments to select environmental protection programmes; it cannot assess the sustainability of economic performance
- *Market instruments* prompt households and enterprises to internalize environmental externalities in their plans and budgets
- Models of *computable general equilibrium* analyse short-term effects of market instruments
- *Optimal growth models* conceptualize sustainable and optimal economic growth; they are less useful for practical policy-making
- *Technology*: problem or solution? Economic analysis is inconclusive
- *Rent capture and reinvestment* are necessary conditions for sustaining economic growth and development

Neo-liberal economists believe that unfettered markets are better at announcing and dealing with environmental problems than the 'conceited blueprints of politicians, the hubris of monopolistic businessmen, or the arrogance of scientists' (*The Economist*, 11 September 1999: 20). Relying on market forces will not do, however, when markets ignore severe environmental externalities.* Externalities, and in particular environmental ones, cause market failure (Chapter 5). Governments intervene, discouraging negative externalities, encouraging positive ones and providing necessary public goods.

Figure 5.7 illustrated the generation of a fictitious market for nature's services; the illustration applies also to the supply of public goods and services by the government, including environmental protection. When more than one project could deal with a particular environmental problem,

cost–benefit analysis helps select the project with the highest net benefit. The illustrative example of Table 7.1 compares the net benefits of a logging ban with continuing deforestation at a Philippine resort. Deforestation would impair tourism and fisheries by generating siltation of coastal waters and damage to the coral reef. On the other hand, the logging ban would reduce timber sales and revenues to zero. The logging ban is the efficient option as it obtains higher revenues over a 10-year period. Note that discounting reduces the current value of revenues, but does not change the general outcome of the analysis.

Cost–benefit analysis of a project or programme does not capture economy-wide optimality, as achieved at least in theory by general equilibrium analysis (Chapter 5, further reading); nor can it assess the contribution of a project to the overall sustainability of the economy. The reason is that implementing a project brings about price and output changes in other projects and sectors that are ignored by particular project analysis. Despite these problems and difficulties of measuring environmental damage (Chapter 5), cost–benefit analysis is still the only way to lift environmental protection programmes out of the irrationality of political negotiation and lobbying.

Environmental economists favour the **internalization of externalities** into the planning and budgets of households and enterprises. They expect environmental cost internalization to restore or at least approach optimality

Table 7.1 Cost–benefit analysis of deforestation: El Nido, Philippines (US$ thousands)

	Option 1: logging ban	Option 2: continued logging	Option 1 minus option 2
Gross revenue (1987–96):			
Tourism	47,415	8,178	39,237
Fisheries	28,070	12,844	15,226
Logging	0	12,885	–12,885
Total	75,485	33,907	41,578
Present value (10% discount rate):			
Tourism	25,481	6,280	19,201
Fisheries	17,248	9,108	8,140
Logging	0	9,769	–9,769
Total	42,729	25,157	17,572

Source: Dixon *et al.* (1994: 45, Table 5), with permission from Taylor & Francis.

in the economy. International organizations (OECD 1989; United Nations 1994) popularized the idea as the polluter-pays principle. The principle simply wants people to be accountable for the environmental damage they cause. Models of computable general equilibrium* claim to find optimal solutions for different scenarios of environmental cost internalization. Standard textbook economics provides the formalization of how markets may (or may not) achieve a new general equilibrium. Broadly, one can distinguish the following policy instruments of environmental cost internalization:

- hard instruments of rules and regulations, which prohibit hazardous products and production and proscribe safe production techniques;
- soft instruments of subsidies, education and information to bring out environmental responsibility and ingenuity in corporations and consumers; and, somewhere in-between,
- semi-soft/hard market instruments of
  - product charges for environmental impacts of production and consumption, and
  - creation of markets for environmental source and sink functions.

Note that these instruments reflect also the strategic attitudes of economic agents tackling environmental limits for production and consumption (Chapter 4). Figure 7.1 lampoons these attitudes and the typical institutional set-up of environmental policy by governments, markets and civil society.

Hard instruments of command and control are rapidly and incisively effective but inefficient in finding the best environmentally sound production and consumption patterns and techniques. Rules and regulations do avoid assessing difficult-to-measure marginal environmental damage required for optimal market intervention (see below). They are judgemental, however, when setting environmental standards or targets. **Soft instruments** seek to elicit and reward voluntary actions and positive non-market effects. The benefits of these effects are difficult to assess; they are also insufficient in offsetting mostly negative externalities.

Market instruments are the classic tools of economics for dealing with externalities and restoring optimality in market behaviour. The idea is to prompt economic agents into budgeting for their environmental impacts. Market instruments are usually aimed at enterprises rather than consumers. In general, enterprises have better knowledge of their impacts and of the techniques and costs of avoiding or reducing them. Market instruments include environmental charges and taxes, and the creation of markets for pollution permits, natural resource quotas and ecosystem services. In the

Figure 7.1 Environmental policy instruments: command and control to enforce compliance with regulations (which governments do); sell and buy after budgeting environmental costs (which markets do); change your lifestyle (which environmentalists call for).

case of uncertain high-risk impacts, refundable deposits could be charged to those suspected or expected to cause the impacts. Figure 7.2 illustrates how a Pigouvian eco-tax (Pigou 1920/1932) can reduce emissions E from the production of a marketed good Q. The challenge is to find the optimal tax rate t so that the price of the good equals its total social (private and external) marginal cost.

The problems of determining marginal environmental costs and benefits for purposes of optimal policy show up in costing the impacts of climate change. Table 7.2 indicates the wide range of marginal damage estimates by different sources. Among the lowest estimates is Nordhaus's **optimal carbon price and tax** of US$7.4 per ton of CO_2 emissions (in 2005). Optimality implies that the marginal damage for the emission of a pollutant equals the marginal benefits of its abatement. In other words, optimality is a prescription for spending on emission reduction until the last dollar spent reduces damage by less than a dollar. The relatively low level of the optimal tax indicates that an economy-wide modelled tax could indeed be more efficient than policies based on simple cost comparisons of environmental action and inaction (Table 5.2). Note that in 2005 the *actual* carbon price of the European Union's Emission Trading System (EU ETS) peaked at about triple the optimal global-policy price of the Nordhaus model. Of course, imperfect real-world conditions and partial coverage of only half of the region's CO_2 emissions are a far cry from the smooth utility and production curves of a globally optimizing economic model.

Political expediencies often obfuscate environmental objectives and the setting of market instruments. For example, in Germany, the proclaimed objective of an **ecological tax reform** is to use the revenues from an

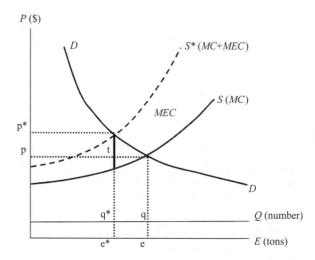

Figure 7.2 Optimal eco-tax. Supply *S* (represented by the marginal cost *MC* of production) and demand *D* determine the market price *p*, output *q* and emission *e* for product *Q*. Adding the marginal cost of an environmental external effect *MEC* to the private marginal cost *MC* yields a new supply curve *S**, which accounts for the total marginal *social cost* of production. Assuming that consumer preferences and the demand function *D* for *Q* remain the same, price p increases to p*, production q decreases to q* and emission e decreases to e*. The optimal eco-tax rate t is equal to the additional marginal damage cost MEC* at the intersection of *S** and *D*. At this point, the total marginal social cost of production MC* + MEC* equals the equilibrium price p*, which in turn reflects the marginal benefits of consuming q*.

eco-tax to reduce labour-related taxes. The result should be a 'double dividend' (Goulder 1995) of taxing a 'bad' (pollution) and relieving the tax burden of a 'good' (labour). The results are questionable, though, because other socio-economic objectives, notably fostering employment in coal-mining states, riddled the reform with exemptions (Bartelmus 2008).

The above policy measures aim to reduce environmental impacts in the short and medium term. Policy-makers might hope for continuation in the long run, but cannot of course ensure implementation beyond legislative mandates. Policies of long-term sustainability also face uncertainties of forecasting and scenario building. But even mainstream economists realized early on that exhaustible natural resources could undermine economic growth. Natural resource economists searched, therefore, for an **optimal extraction schedule** over the lifetime of an exhaustible resource.*

Table 7.2 Marginal cost of climate change

	Marginal damage costs ($/tCO$_2$)	Marginal abatement costs ($/tCO$_2$)
IPCC (2007b)	12[a]	35[b] (5–65)
Stern (2006)	85[c]	
Nordhaus (2008)	7.4[d] (2.6–12.0)	7.4–54[e]
EU ETS (Ellerman and Joskow 2008)		30[f]
World Bank (2006)	5.5–28[g]	

Notes:
a   Average peer-reviewed estimates in 2005.
b   Mean of range for 550 ppm CO_2 equivalent stabilization goal in 2100.
c   Marginal social carbon costs, including 'risks' in 2006.
d   Social cost of no-emission-control scenario in 2005 (with uncertainty range).
e   Optimal eco-tax in 2005, increasing to $54 in 2100.
f   Highest actual carbon (dioxide) price in 2005 of the European Union's Emission Trading System (EU ETS).
g   Marginal global damage, 1991–2030.

Neo-liberal economists expressed their *laissez-faire* view of the relationship between environmental impact and economic growth in the **environmental Kuznets curve** hypothesis. Economist Simon Kuznets (1955) found an inverted-U relationship between the level and distribution of income. Grossman and Krueger (1995) detected a similar relationship between environmental quality and economic growth. Their hypothesis is that industrializing countries generate initially high and increasing environmental impacts. Once these countries reach a certain level of prosperity, greater demand for environmental quality and the transition to a dematerialized service economy reverse the initial correlation of environmental deterioration and economic growth (Figure 7.3, part A). Other empirical analyses indicate that this relationship holds only for a few local pollutants. Some even see a relinkage of environmental impact and economic growth (Figure 7.3, part B). Any permanent improvement of environmental quality would then be a matter of deliberate environmental policy, rather than the automatic result of economic growth (Barbier 1997).

Rejecting the environmental Kuznets curve hypothesis means that ignoring long-term environmental impacts is not an option. Economists therefore introduce natural capital and environmental quality in models of **optimal and sustainable economic growth**. Their objective is to maximize not only current but also future income and output, taking environmental damage and the depletion of natural capital into account. Depending on assumptions about technological progress and substitution of exhaustible resources the models determine maximum infinitely sustainable final consumption.* Two

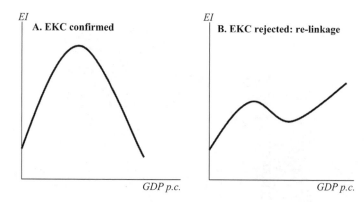

Figure 7.3 Environmental Kuznets curve (EKC), confirmed and rejected. Part A shows the inverted-U relationship of the EKC hypothesis: environmental impact (*EI*) increases with economic growth at low levels of *GDP per capita* and decreases after the economy reaches a certain level of income and wealth. Part B illustrates a relinkage of environmental deterioration with economic growth after an initial EKC effect.

Source: Bartelmus (2008: 199, Figure 11.1), with kind permission from Springer Science+ Business Media B.V.

issues affect model results, in particular; one is the choice of the discount rate, the other is the role of technological progress.

Nordhaus's (2008) optimizing model of economic growth and climate change applies a **market-oriented discount rate** of 4 per cent to the values of climate damage and control. It is a good example of how economists assess future and uncertain environmental damage and the investments to reduce it (Figure 7.4). A gradual increase in the optimal eco-tax rates from US$7.4 in 2005 to US$55 in 2100 is expected to deal efficiently with projected increases of CO_2 concentration in the atmosphere.

Anticipating catastrophic events and citing ethical reasons of inter-generational equity (Chapter 5), environmentalists favour low **social discounting**. They tend to magnify potential impacts, reversing the high-discounting view of Figure 7.4. Consequently, they oppose a gradualist policy course and demand strong action now (e.g. Stern 2006). Ecological economists also argue that high damage costs overwhelm marginal economic analysis. Just imagine what the total social cost of nuclear energy production would be if it included insurance for a major nuclear accident at low or zero discount rates (cf. Figure 5.5). Perhaps surprisingly, a main-stream economist, Weitzman (2009), supports this view. He uses formal cost–benefit analysis to show the 'contentiously subjective' results of economic analysis for highly uncertain but potentially catastrophic

Figure 7.4 Economic discounting: should he reverse his telescope?

climate change events; his conclusion is to avoid 'presenting a cost-benefit estimate… as if it is accurate and objective' (Weitzman 2009: 18). Nordhaus (2008: 147) counters: 'we should start with the clear and present dangers, after which we can turn to the unclear and distant threats'.

Besides the highly judgemental setting of discount rates, economic growth models also differ greatly in their assumptions about the role of **technology** (Figure 7.5).* For instance, Koopmans (1973) demonstrates the feasibility of sustaining optimal growth with the help of technological progress, while Islam (2001) shows that ecological limits curb economic growth. A common finding is the need to maintain the value of produced and natural capital as one condition for sustainability. This corroborates the sustainability measures of integrated environmental-economic accounting (Chapter 6). However, optimal growth models show a high degree of abstraction with questionable assumptions about utility maximization, substitution of production factors, markets in equilibrium and technological progress. They help define economic–environmental sustainability as capital maintenance, but do not provide realistic policy advice.

Rather than filtering data through mathematical constructs, policy-makers might be well advised to look directly at the facts and figures of the past. The closest economics can get to analysis without entering abstract modelling are the national accounts. These are designed to measure the variables of economic analysis in terms of observable indicators. Integrated environmental-economic accounts (Chapter 6) expand this measurement for the assessment of economic sustainability as capital maintenance.

Figure 7.5 Technology the saviour? Or the culprit of environmental deterioration? Models of sustainable economic growth are inconclusive.

Analysis which stays close to these accounts makes for a realistic sustainability economics. Lacking knowledge about the significance of critical irreplaceable natural capital (Chapter 3), policy-makers will have to rely on this benchmark of weak sustainability.

Resource-rich developing countries, in particular, should focus on the efficient management of their natural wealth. Costing and taxing the depletion of their wealth would not only change individual behaviour but also generate revenue for the government. **Rent capture** by taxing the profits of resource-exploiting industries and reinvesting the rents would turn natural wealth into productive capital. Otherwise, the blessing of natural resource endowment might easily turn into a 'resource curse' of missed development and worse.* Figure 7.6 illustrates the success and failure of rent capture in two southern African countries.

One type of modelling stands out because of its close connection to the national accounts: input–output analysis is based on input–output tables, which display the supply and use of goods and services in a detailed inter-industry account. Input–output tables and analyses reveal connections between ecological and environmental economics; they might show the way (explored next) to a common theory of sustainability economics.

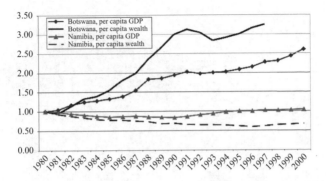

Figure 7.6 Rent capture and economic growth in Botswana and Namibia. High rent capture (by taxation of 76 per cent of resource rents) and investment in produced capital made for high per-capita growth in produced and natural wealth and GDP in Botswana. Namibia captured much less of its rents, and its total wealth declined; the result is non-sustainability of declining productive capital and a stagnating economy.

Source: Lange (2004: Figure 3), with kind permission from Springer Science+Business Media B.V.

Want to know more?

Ecological economists hold that, besides monopolies and other **market imperfections**, irreversible and disastrous environmental effects render the marginal analysis of economic optimality irrelevant (Funtowicz and Ravetz 1991; Daly 1996). In defence, economists argue that a theoretical 'vacuum' can provide valuable insight into complex problems (Samuelson and Nordhaus 1992: 295), and a 'sequence of policy reforms' in less-than-perfect situations will still help to increase overall economic welfare (Dasgupta 1994: 42). The stalwart of neo-liberal market economics, *The Economist*, asserts that 'markets often correct their own failures' (17 February 1996, 'Schools brief': 64).

Computable general equilibrium (CGE) models link micro-economic optimizing behaviour of utility and profit maximization to macro-economic analysis. They show the effects of policy measures such as environmental standards or market instruments. Comparative-static models predict the changes in economic variables from the original equilibrium to the new one, resulting from micro-economic responses to governmental policies. Conrad (1999) reviews the methods and applications of environmental CGE models. CGE models obtain their computability from using national accounts and input–output statistics (Chapters 6, 8) for a more or less detailed breakdown of economic activities. They still suffer from unrealistic assumptions of perfect market conditions and smooth (mathematical) production and utility functions. Most textbooks of environmental economics stay with this micro-oriented approach to dealing with environmental externalities and natural resource depletion.

Natural resource economics is a special branch of conventional economics. It established the rules for the optimal exploitation of an exhaustible natural resource like coal or oil. Maximizing the return from the use of such a resource requires its unit rent (the net price, calculated as the market price minus the unit extraction cost) to be increased at the prevailing interest rate. This so-called Hotelling (1931) rule ensures continuing market clearance for the supply and demand of the resource at market prices. Up to now, natural resource economics remains a part of conventional market analysis.

Applying a social discount rate instead of the prevailing interest rate for the sake of conserving a natural resource for future generations extends natural resource economics into the non-economic sphere of sustainability and inter-generational equity (Chapter 5). Solow (1974) presents a clear and non-mathematical review of narrow resource economics and broader sustainability analysis of natural resource use. Most textbooks on environmental economics claim natural resource economics as part of their subject area (e.g. Tietenberg 2005).

Auty (1993) characterized the failure to turn natural (mineral) wealth into economic growth and development as the 'resource curse'. Reasons for this failure include volatility of resource prices and currency rates, use of resource rent for consumption rather than investment, and social conflict and corruption in resource-rich countries.

Under the influence of the international discussion of sustainable development (Chapter 9), economists expanded natural resource economics to include broadly defined natural capital and environmental damage. **Optimal and sustainable growth models** are the result; they incorporate environmental damage into a social welfare function and maximize national welfare under natural capital constraints (Solow 1974; Dasgupta and Mäler 1991, 2000; Arrow *et al.* 2004). Aware of the rather unrealistic assumption of perfect market conditions, Arrow *et al.*

(2003) show that sustainability can replace optimality for modelling the growth of imperfect economies. They still remain, however, in the realm of conceptualizing theory. As Nordhaus (2008: 80) succinctly observes for his own climate model, the results of such models 'convey a spurious precision', but are at least 'internally consistent'. Munasinghe's (2002) reader provides a rare overview of green macro-economics. Undaunted by the problems of global modelling, UNEP's (2011b) simulation of a green economy takes an optimistic view of increasing or restoring natural capital. A relatively small investment of 2 per cent of global GDP would not only generate greater global wealth and economic growth, but also reduce poverty because natural capital services benefit the poor.

Chapter 3 referred to the power of **technological progress** to reduce the input of primary materials from the environment. Such dematerialization could be the result of a transition to a post-industrial service economy, hailed at the time by popular magazines as the advent of a permanently growing new economy; see, for example, *Time*, 30 May 1983 <http://www.time.com/time/magazine/article/0,9171,926013-1,00.html> (accessed on 19 June 2011); *Newsweek*, 4 August 1997 <http://www.newsweek.com/1997/08/03/the-new-rich.html> (accessed on 19 June 2011). A 'new growth theory' explained this optimistic outlook as a matter of driving technological innovation 'endogenously' by a deliberate promotion of knowledge through research and development, rather than relying on exogenous accidental discovery (Cortright 2001).

New information and communication technology (ICT) has been a key player in technological progress. International organizations promote the new technologies for development by assessing case studies in developing and transition economies (World Bank 2003a) and by a Global Alliance for Information and Communication Technologies and Development (United Nations 2009–2010). The European Union is attempting to attain a 'digital revolution' by 2020 (European Commission, Information Society n.d.). Recessions in rich countries may now have dampened the enthusiasm for the new economy. Indeed, ICT lost some of its lustre: high energy inputs, and short life and use of ICT hardware have somewhat offset undeniable gains in productivity, dematerialization and detoxification of economic activities (Elliot 2007).

Points for discussion

- What's wrong with markets? Why can't they deal with natural resource depletion, environmental degradation and environmental protection?
- Governments fail, too. Can cost–benefit analysis of their programmes and projects help?
- Can internalizing environmental externalities bring back optimality in production and consumption? How?
- Does economic growth improve environmental quality? Check the validity of the EKC hypothesis.
- Nordhaus's optimal growth model determines the optimal global eco-tax for CO_2 emissions. Is this the best way to balance climate change effects with the benefits of economic growth? Can the model deal with catastrophic events?
- Does green accounting provide better cost data for setting market instruments than modelled (optimal) cost calculations?
- How should governments use eco-tax revenues: for reducing labour cost, for environmental protection, or as they see fit (for the common good)?
- Can/will technology ensure the sustainability of our economies?
- Is endowment with natural resources a curse or a blessing?

8 Bridging the gap
Ecological and environmental economics

- Pessimistic assessments of environmental disaster and optimistic trust in markets are at the roots of *dissent* between ecological and environmental economists
- *Physical input–output tables* and *hybrid accounts* connect environmental impacts to economic activity; they do not measure sustainability
- *Input–output and general equilibrium models* set environmental standards for economic activities; they could assess short-term sustainability
- *Models of optimal sustainable growth* clarify the meaning of intergenerational equity and sustainable welfare; they remain in the realm of abstract welfare economics
- *Linear programming* optimizes bounded economic activity; it points to a common operational theory of ecological and environmental sustainability

---

Throughout Parts 1 and 2 we have compared the different views of ecological and environmental economists. The crude distinction between **eco-centric ecological and anthropocentric environmental economics** is of course a simplification of different schools of thought on greening economics (Chapter 1). It is, however, real enough to differentiate between rather pessimistic biophysical assessments of environmentalists and more optimistic economic analysis of environmental problems. As discussed in Chapters 3 and 6, different strengths of sustainability capture this disparity in more operational terms. Ecological economists call for strong sustainability as a way of living within the limits of nature's carrying capacities. In contrast, environmental economists claim that weak sustainability of maintaining the value of produced and natural capital can balance environmental costs and benefits with economic ones.

Both schools recognize impacts of economic production and consumption as the causes of environmental deterioration. They differ in their view of what should be primarily sustained: the environment or the economy. The question is whether one can replace 'or' by 'and'. In other words, can we **bridge** the different approaches to defining, measuring and attaining **ecological and economic sustainability**? Is there a way to combine the findings of ecological and environmental economics in unified analysis and policy? A two-pronged approach (Figure 8.1) could provide answers by introducing

- the biophysical indicators of ecological economics into economic accounts, and
- ecological norms and standards into economic analysis.

Disdain for economic growth appears to be the reason why ecological economists tend to ignore economic values in their assessments of the state and trend of the environment. A promising way of introducing economic activities in these assessments could be to open the black box of the economy in material flow accounts (Chapter 2). Input–output tables do just this by presenting inter-industry flows of physical commodities in full consistency with the national accounts.* Environmentally extended physical and hybrid (monetary–physical) input–output tables can indeed connect ecological and economic data in a common accounting framework.

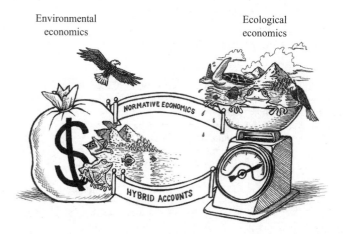

Figure 8.1 Bridging the gap? A two-pronged approach could introduce physical impact data into economic accounts, on the one hand, and ecological norms and limits into environmental economics, on the other hand. Hybrid (physical–monetary) accounts and normative economics would be the result.

Physical input–output tables (PIOTs) represent the physical counterpart of supply and use in the monetary national accounts. Extended
versions show natural resource flows into different sectors of the economy
and residual discharges from these sectors into the environment. This
allows environmental source and sink services to be related directly to their
economic uses. Input–output tables are, however, rarely compiled in purely
physical form because of costly data requirements. Table 8.1 shows the one-
shot German PIOT in an aggregate format. The table adds about 50 billion
tons of materials and residuals to the conventional (physical) input–output
table. Nature's input of primary materials into the economy amounts to 49.6
billion tons, and the economy's output of residuals into nature 49.1 billion
tons. The difference is accumulated in durable goods and inventories.

The results of these additions are obscure: what are we to make of a
total material flow in the economy of 113 billion tons or a physical GDP of
3.9 billion tons? Note that the physical GDP excludes non-material services,
whose increasing significance characterizes the post-industrial stage of economic development. Obviously, the aggregation in tons, not only of apples
and oranges but also of machines, buildings and computers, cannot reflect the
different values of goods and services for human use. Expanding the material
flow accounts to include economic activities in physical terms fails, therefore,
to provide a meaningful evaluation of economic performance and its interaction with the environment. Nonetheless, the revised green accounting system
of the United Nations (Committee of Exports on Environmental Economic
Accounting 2012) appears to focus on these physical flows (Chapter 6).

Relating physical environmental data directly to the monetary economic
indicators of the national accounts might yield better results. The Dutch
National Accounting Matrix including Environmental Accounts (NAMEA)

Table 8.1 Physical input–output table, Germany, 1990 (billion tons)

Output (supply)	Input (use)			
	Intermediate uses	Final uses		Total material use
	By the economy (industries)	By the economy (GDP)	By nature (residuals)	
Industries	7.6	3.6	48.3	59.5
Households	2.8		0.8	3.6
Nature	49.3	0.3		49.6
Total material supply	59.7	3.9	49.1	112.7

Source: Stahmer *et al.* (1998: Table 12), modified and aggregated.

(de Haan and Kee n.d.) is a **hybrid input–output table**. It maintains the monetary supply and use accounts and places physical flows of natural resources and emissions next to the monetary transactions. Figure 8.2 is thus similar to the PIOT (Table 8.1), except for its white core of conventional monetary accounting. The figure also explicitly includes transboundary physical and monetary flows to and from the rest of the world. NAMEA avoids any changes in the economic national accounts as it 'maintains a strict borderline between the economic sphere and the natural environment' (de Haan and Kee n.d.: 2). The NAMEA accountants see this as strength. Bordering up the economy, however, thwarts a genuine comparison of economic outcomes with environmental impacts, and hence a truly integrative assessment of ecological and economic sustainability. This may actually be the intention of the SEEA revision, as most national accountants oppose fully merging environmental data in national accounts indicators (Chapter 6).

USE (by) / SUPPLY (of)	*Industries 1, 2, ...*	*Final demand*			*PHYSICAL material flows (natural resources, residuals)*
		Households	*Capital formation and accumulation*	*Rest of the World (ROW)*	
Outputs (including imports)	Intermediate consumption	Final consumption	Capital formation	Exports	*Emissions from industries and households*
Income	Value added, NDP				
Rest of the World (ROW)	Imports		Capital transfer to ROW	Balance of payments	*Imports of natural resources and residuals*
PHYSICAL material flows (natural resources, residuals)	*Natural resource inputs, residuals received*	*Natural resource use, 'consumption' of residuals*	*Net accumulation of materials and substances*	*Exports of natural resources and residuals*	*Physical balances*

Figure 8.2 Simplified structure of NAMEA. The hybrid input–output system shows the physical supply and use of natural resources and pollutants (residuals) next to the monetary accounting indicators of supply and use of goods and services. The NAMEA is thus an intermediate step only towards integrative environmental-economic accounting; it could provide, though, the database for hybrid models of physical environmental impacts from economic activity.

Source: based on Bartelmus (2004: 49, Table II), with permission from Elsevier.

Physical and hybrid accounts do not build good bridges between ecological and economic assessments. Less rigid but assumption-laden models could be more successful. **Hybrid models** have indeed come up with policy options that take particular physical environmental targets into account. Figure 8.3 combines, for illustrative purposes, two versions of a hybrid input–output model. The original model focused on the environmental placeholder, CO_2 emission, by means of an eco-tax (Meyer 1999). The newer model takes the success of the European Union's climate policy for granted and tests the increase in natural resource productivity (Chapter 3) as the main environmental policy (Meyer 2005). The eco-tax model slowed GDP growth and reduced CO_2 emission, whereas dematerialization is expected to bring about economic 'vitalization' (Meyer 2005: 20) and stronger GDP growth.

Computable general equilibrium (CGE) models also combine physical environmental impacts with more or less disaggregated monetary input–output tables. However, CGE models determine equilibrium prices as a result of optimal behaviour by economic agents (Chapter 7). Note that the above input–output model just added environmental costs as 'mark-ups' to existing price levels. CGE models typically define environmental policy in terms of emission standards that should not be exceeded. Economists

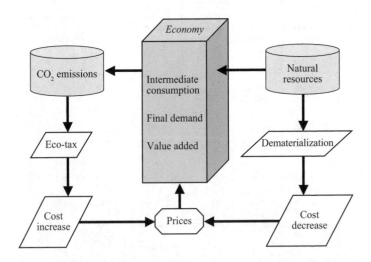

Figure 8.3 Hybrid input–output model. The German *Panta Rhei* model (Meyer 1999, 2005) uses monetary and physical input–output data and national accounts indicators. This radically reduced sketch illustrates the introduction of physical CO_2 emissions from, and natural resource use by, industries and households. Increased cost of an emission-related tax and decreased cost of natural-resource-saving dematerialization change relative prices and the structure and level of the economy.

dispute such mixing of observable real-world data with judgemental norms (Chapter 9). However, the main drawbacks of CGE models are their unrealistic assumptions of competitive markets and mathematical production, consumption and utility functions that maximize welfare in a general equilibrium of the economy. Moreover, they are basically static in nature and do not normally show the transition from one equilibrium to another (future or desirable) one.

Models of optimal economic growth seek to overcome the stasis and the relatively short outlook of input–output and general equilibrium models. However, they suffer from similarly unrealistic assumptions about welfare maximization and its dynamics. One can see, on the other hand, their power of conceptualizing sustainable welfare and its determinants. Chapter 7 showed that environmental economists discount the cost of future environmental impacts, whereas ecological economists favour low or zero discounting for the sake of inter-generational equity. Adjusting the lever of the discount rate could be one way to find a compromise between caring about future generations and seeking prosperity through economic growth.

A more realistic and transparent approach is to combine input–output analysis – based on accounting and input–output statistics – with long-term environmental capacities that pose limits to economic growth. The result would be a clearly defined framework, within which economic activities could play out and could be assessed in terms of quantifiable input–output relationships. This is the approach of **linear programming**.* Figure 8.4 illustrates, for a two-commodity economy, how ecological limits and social requirements (for meeting basic needs) can be set for economic activities. Inequalities, rather than equations, specify (1) environmental limits of maximum use ('no more than') of natural resources and environmental sinks (as permissible pollution), and (2) minimum consumption ('at least as much as') of goods and services to meet standards of living. Linear programming thus determines a feasibility space, where economic activities can be conducted within the limits of carrying capacities of a nation or region (Chapter 3).

Linear programming introduces physical (carrying capacity) constraints for economic activities; it also combines these limits with economic valuation and optimization by weighting (multiplying) physical outputs with monetary unit values in the maximizing function Z^* of Figure 8.4.* The result is a transparent connection of ecological sustainability with the economic analysis of maximum value added and its sum total, net domestic product. Dynamic versions of the model can introduce capital formation by reserving some output for future use. Connecting the – limited – availability of produced and natural capital with optimal capital formation allows ecological sustainability of environmental constraints to be combined with economic sustainability of capital maintenance. The bounded optimality analysis of dynamic linear (and non-linear) programming thus shows us a way

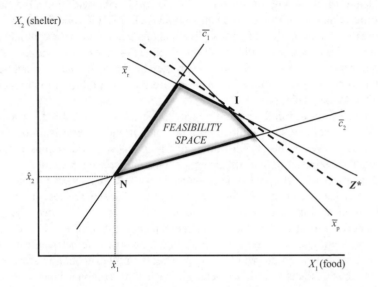

X_2 (shelter)

Figure 8.4 Linear programming of ecologically sustainable and optimal economic activities. Food and shelter production and consumption represent the economy in this illustrative presentation. Linear inequalities of minimum requirements for food $\bar{c}_1$ and shelter $\bar{c}_2$, and standards for maximum use of a natural resource $\bar{x}_r$ and maximum emission of a pollutant $\bar{x}_p$ define the (bold-bordered) feasibility space for economic outputs x_1 and x_2. $\hat{x}_1$ and $\hat{x}_2$ (at point N) are the minimum feasible outputs that meet minimum standards of living represented by $\bar{c}_1$ and $\bar{c}_2$ constraints. Z^* (dashed line) represents the highest net value for the feasible (ecologically sustainable) combinations of food and shelter at the tangent point I.

Source: Bartelmus (2008), Figure 12.3, based on Bartelmus (1979), with kind permission from Springer Science+Business Media B.V.

towards **reconciling ecological and environmental economics** via their sustainability notions.

Combining the two sustainability concepts still requires consensus on the nature and level of environmental constraints. The divisive devil is in the specification of the necessary constraints. Ecological economists would like to curb economic activity to a sustainable physical scale (Chapter 4). Environmental economists would let human preferences weigh the significance and cost of environmental hazards against the benefits of economic production and consumption (Chapter 7). Possibly for these reasons, the linear programming approach to environment–economy interaction has so far been ignored in nation-wide sustainability analysis and policy-making.

We may have found a bridge for unifying ecological and environmental economics. But will environmental and ecological economists cross the bridge and perhaps meet halfway? With few exceptions, both camps seem to ignore each other. In fact, a frequently raised criticism of stressing the polarization of environmental and ecological economics is that it overstates the antagonism between the two camps. Belittling an obvious disagreement is unfortunate, though. It prevents the reciprocal evaluation of normative assessments of biophysical data, on the one hand, and of more positivist environmental-economic analyses, on the other hand. Such evaluation is not meant to stir up antagonism. Raising awareness of divisive issues should foster dialogue rather than dissent between environmentalists and economists.

Want to know more?

Nobel Prize laureate Wassily Leontief (1951) pioneered **input–output analysis**. Input–output analysis explains the structure of the economy as a physical flow system, in which each industry may provide inputs into any other industry. Simple matrix algebra can then determine how much of the outputs of other (antecedent) industries is needed to produce a particular product. Leontief (1970) also introduced pollution and pollution control into his model. Underlying such analysis is an **input–output table** in physical or monetary units of measurement. Monetizing the input–output tables permits presenting inter-industry flows as an integral part of the supply and use accounts of the national accounts (European Commission *et al.* 2009). Hoekstra and van den Bergh (2006) describe different attempts at computing physical input–output tables by European countries. The input–output analyses of Murray and Wood (2010) also stay in the physical realm of ecological economics: they present case studies of the direct and indirect discharge of wastes and pollutants in production. Despite their claim to offer 'the sustainability practitioner's guide', the case studies do not assess the sustainability of economic activity.

Linear programming of economic activities – hence sometimes called activity analysis – opens the input–output system to optimal behaviour under constraints of maximum productive and environmental capacities and minimum consumption requirements. The model determines optimality as the highest monetary value of feasible net output combinations, weighted by value added (v) per unit of output. The tangent value Z^* (for different values of $Z = v_1x_1 + v_2x_2$) in Figure 8.4 represents the maximum feasible and 'greened' net domestic product of an economy operating under environmental (and other) constraints. Refinements of the model allow for non-linear substitution of production factors in dynamic models. Dorfman *et al.* (1958) is still one of the best introductions to the economic analysis of linear programming. Bartelmus (1979) introduced United Nations concepts of inner (social) and outer (environmental) limits into the linear programming framework. So far, however, most empirical applications of linear programming have focused on local ecosystems and corporate management rather than national policies.

Points for discussion

- Is dissent between ecological and environmental economics exaggerated?
- Can linking environmental impact data to economic activities overcome this dissent?
- What can hybrid models do for comparing and combining economic and ecological sustainability?
- How promising is linear programming for combining environmental limits and economic activities?
- Is choosing a relatively low discount rate for future environmental impacts a good compromise between equity for future generations and equity within the present generation?
- Do we need a unifying theory of *eco*-nomics (Chapter 1) with a common sustainability concept?

Part 3

Sustainable development

What else do we need?

9   A cure-all paradigm?

- Sustainable development is an alluring but hazy paradigm
- Like development, *sustainable development* seeks to improve the living conditions of people, but with a focus on the social, economic and environmental needs of current and future generations
- Ecological economists embrace the *normative paradigm*; environmental economists tend to treat sustainable development as a *metaphor* for social progress with environmental conservation
- *Indices of sustainable development* rank countries in terms of indicator averages; they do not define and measure sustainable development
- The *globalization* debate revived sustainable development; it is not clear, however, whether globalization helps or hinders sustainable development

Sustainable development is like the Holy Grail: it appeals to everyone, many believe in its powers, but no one has found it yet. Governments subscribe to sustainable development in Earth Summits (Chapter 10) and at home. The United Nations includes it in its Millennium Development Goals.* The European Union made sustainable development part of its Constitution, as did the hardly environment-minded World Trade Organization (WTO). Few publications on environment and/or development can resist summoning up the concept in support of their arguments. In reality, economic policy continues to focus on economic growth and employment, with environmental agencies on the sidelines (Figure 9.1).

So what makes sustainable development so endearing and elusive at the same time? The answer lies in the cornucopian concept of **development**. Broadly, socio-economic development seeks to improve the living conditions and well-being of people. Obviously such a definition applies to countries at any development stage, including those that may count themselves among

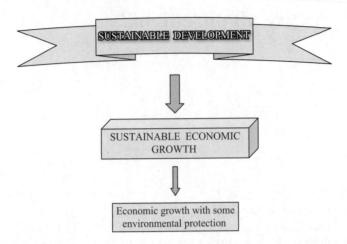

Figure 9.1 Sustainable development – in reductionist mode? Under the banner of sustainable development most countries focus on economic performance and growth: they equate development with economic growth and sustainability with environmental protection.

the developed ones. Attempts at substantiating development refer to a large variety of human needs and less tangible aspirations (Max-Neef *et al.* 1989). Deficiencies in meeting even 'basic needs' (International Labour Organization 1977) characterize the situation in developing countries. Figure 9.2 indicates – in terms of comparative rankings by the Human Development

Figure 9.2 Least and most developed countries according to the Human Development Index 2010. The index ranks countries by an average of per-capita gross national income, literacy and life expectancy. Note that in terms of GNI per capita Liechtenstein would come out first; on the other hand, GNI per capita would lower New Zealand and Ireland to rank 33 and 25, respectively. The ten least developed countries are all in Africa.

Index (UNDP 2010) – the low development situation in Africa and high development of North America, Europe and Oceania.

Frustration with lost Development Decades of International Development Strategies* and conspicuous environmental decline prompted the United Nations to establish a World Commission on Environment and Development (WCED). The objective was to investigate the reasons for the failures of environmental and developmental policies, and to suggest solutions. The Commission called for **sustainable development*** as the concept for integrating fragmented policies of specialized departments and agencies. Policy integration would deal more effectively with cross-cutting 'spill-over' effects of programmes and projects on poverty and environment. Sustainable development thus adds a further 'pillar' (United Nations 2003) of environmental protection to those of social justice and economic growth, commonly identified with economic development; institution building is also often identified as a fourth pillar (Figure 9.3). The pillar metaphor seems to come close to the support function of capital in sustainable economic

Figure 9.3 The four pillars of sustainable development. Interacting economic, environmental, social and institutional policies need to be integrated or at least coordinated. According to the World Commission on Environment and Development, governmental departments and agencies tend to act independently, which caused the failure of both environmental and developmental strategies.

growth (Chapter 6). Others prefer to speak of three or four 'dimensions' of sustainable development, stressing the need for integrating development goals (e.g. UNESCO n.d.).

The World Commission also advanced the popular **definition of sustainable development** as 'development that meets the needs of the present without compromising the ability of future generations to meet their own needs' (WCED 1987: 43). Meeting the needs of future generations is a matter of equity in the inter-generational distribution of income and produced and natural wealth. Inter-generational equity is to make sure that future generations will enjoy at least the same level of prosperity and environmental amenities as the present generation. For the present generation, intra- and international equity refers to the social dimension of development. The objective is to reduce the gap in wealth and welfare within countries and between rich and poor countries. One can assume that human needs include these and all other development goals.

The wide range of needs turns the paradigm into an alluring but hazy aspiration: everyone can subscribe to it without risk of being held accountable for its success or failure. To industry, sustainable development might offer opportunities for investing in environmental protection; governments adopt it to pacify environmentalist objections to economic growth; and civil society uses it to argue against globalization. With sustainable development 'all [is] in harmony' (WCED 1987: 46).

Such harmony augurs well for **reconciling environmentalist and economic worldviews**, where measurement and modelling seem to fail (Chapter 8). Ecological economics is characterized by moralistic calls for frugality, environmental responsibility and social justice (Chapter 4). It is therefore not surprising that ecological economists co-opted a paradigm that is 'based on social values and ethical norms' (Faucheux 2001: 1763) and caters to 'qualitative development' rather than quantitative economic growth (Daly and Farley 2004: 6). 'Co-evolutionary economics' represents an institutional view of ecological economics (Söderbaum 1999; Faucheux 2001): it uses the ecological notion of evolution to address changes in values and institutions necessary for sustaining environment and development in the long term. Institutional reform is expected to sustain all pillars of development.

Perhaps less normative, but equally broad and vague, is the utility-based notion of welfare. Both environmentalists and economists use welfare to denote positive effects of well-being from ecosystem services, the consumption of goods and services and other social and cultural amenities. Welfare maximization and development objectives are thus equivalent at a higher metaphysical level – as compared to the more down-to-earth links between environmental limits and outputs of economic activities (Chapters 4, 8). Dissent sets in when evaluating the welfare effects and setting priorities for environmental and/or economic policies (Figure 9.4) Mainstream economists see the mixing of ecological and social norms and facts as an obstruction of scientific analysis. In their view, social values and norms are institutional pre-conditions that should not blur scientific (fact-based) economics (Samuelson and Nordhaus 1992; Beckerman 1994). Ecological economists Krall and Klitgaard (2007: 185, 190) counter that 'ecological economics must extricate itself from [its] neoclassical roots' since it 'is better served by institutional economics and heterodox political economy'.

Environmental economists are less categorical about combining environmental standards and economic analysis. They are still uneasy, though, about dealing with the popular paradigm of sustainable development. Their textbooks might devote a chapter or two to sustainable development, treating the subject as a matter of **strong versus weak sustainability** (e.g. Turner *et al.* 1993; Tietenberg 2005; Hanley *et al.* 2007; see also Chapters 3 and 6 above). Adopting weak economic sustainability allows sustainable development to be considered as economic growth, since all types of capital (or pillars) are

Figure 9.4 Harmony in the clouds – dissent on earth. Sustainable development promises abundance and is vague enough to be generally accepted. Environmentalists and economists fail to agree, though, on setting priorities for and implementing policies of environmental protection and economic growth.

assumed to be substitutable. Ecological economists dispute this assumption; they argue that irreplaceable critical natural capital might bring down economic growth and welfare. Environmental economists might not deny the existence of 'complementary' (non-substitutable) natural capital but would leave its preservation to the conservationism of environmentalists. Similarly, they tend to leave other social, cultural or political development concerns to separate disciplines of institutional and development economics.

Ecological economists seek to fill the normative concept with substance by selecting representative indicators for the different pillars of sustainable development. Particular indicators can warn us about positive or negative trends in the fields they represent. Their linking to targets and standards would make the vision of sustainable development more visible. However, such linkage makes the vision highly judgemental. Chapter 2 referred to some of the international indicator frameworks for assessing sustainable development. The frameworks may bring some order to lengthy indicator lists but do not remove the problems of indicator selection and aggregation. Despite these problems, popular **indices of sustainable development*** claim to:

- show 'progress... toward sustainable development' (Sustainable Development Index: Nováček and Mederly 2002: 50);
- assess the sustainability of society and its 'good life' in terms of high levels of 'human and ecosystem well-being' (Well-Being Index: Prescott-Allen 2001: 1);
- gauge the 'prospects for long-term environmental sustainability' (Environmental Sustainability Index: Yale Center for Environmental Law and Policy and Center for International Earth Science Information Network 1997–2006: 1).

All these indices can do is to compare the ranks of countries. The reason is that indicator averages cannot define the levels of overall sustainability and development. Figure 9.5 shows that rankings may vary considerably because of differences in scope, coverage and indicator selection. All in all, indicators and indices offer neither a clear definition of sustainable development, nor a blueprint for implementation.

The **globalization** debate and demonstrations at ministerial meetings of the WTO in Seattle, Cancún and Hong Kong revived sustainable development as an alternative to globalizing capitalism. More than any other institution, the WTO embodies such capitalism through its promotion of free trade in competitive international markets. Negative social and environmental effects of globalization make the WTO something of a red rag for environmentalists. This is despite WTO's constitutional subscription to sustainable development.*

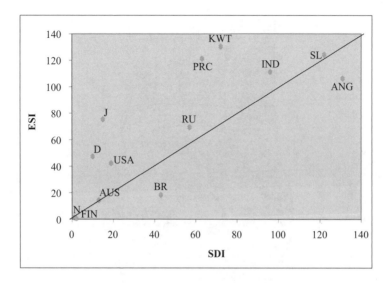

Figure 9.5 Sustainable development ranking of selected countries. On a scale of
1 to 131 (for the countries included in the ranking), the Sustainable
Development Index (SDI) and the more forward-looking Environmental
Sustainability Index (ESI) show diverging results. Exceptions are top-
ranked countries Norway, Finland and Australia, and low-ranked Sierra
Leone. Angola and Kuwait are lowest (at 131) according to the SDI
and ESI, respectively. Country codes: ANG – Angola, AUS – Australia,
BR – Brazil, D – Germany, FIN – Finland, IND – India, J – Japan,
KWT – Kuwait, PRC – China, RU – Russia, SL – Sierra Leone.

Source: Bartelmus (2008, Table 5.4), selected countries.

Globalization is not new. Proselytizing colonialism spread Western
faith and civilization, established the political dominance of European
countries, and supported their economic growth and industrialization
(Figure 9.6). What changed are the speed and nature of the interaction of
countries and their trade. It is not clear whether globalization helps or hinders sustainable development.* For economists, trade liberalization makes
use of the comparative advantages of countries in knowledge and produced
and natural capital endowment. The resulting acceleration of economic
growth improves standards of living and environmental protection in all
nations. Globalization also helps, in their view, to spread the message of
sustainable development and corresponding social and environmental
standards. Environmentalists believe that the social costs of growth triggered by foreign trade drown out comparative advantage; they also fear that

Figure 9.6 Globalization is not new. In the nineteenth and early twentieth century, windjammers and clippers crossed the oceans to bring natural resources and exotic products to European countries.

unbridled competition from trade liberalization causes the abandonment of social, cultural and environmental achievements.

Sustainable development may take the high road of reminding politicians of non-material social goals, and in particular the inequitable treatment of the current and future generations. But can it handle the low ground of practical environmental and socio-economic policy-making?

Want to know more?

Since the 1960s, the United Nations has sought to improve the standards of living of developing countries through a number of **International Development Strategies**, presented and monitored in Development Decades. However, despite a return to economic growth (with added social and environmental objectives) in the fourth and last decade, the strategies failed to reduce the gap between rich and poor countries (Bartelmus 1994). The **Millennium Development Goals** (MDG) of the United Nations (2010b) now set targets for old and a few new (AIDS, globalization) development concerns. The goals include poverty, education, gender equality, health, environmental sustainability, and global partnership for development. In 2010 a UN Summit, 'expressing deep concern' that progress 'falls short of what is needed' (United Nations 2010a: para. 1), issued a new 'action agenda' to meet the goals by their 2015 deadline. However, the MDG seem to skirt economic growth and look more like an agenda for social development. It remains to be seen whether such a narrow development concept can be more successful than the more comprehensive strategies of the Development Decades.

Sustainable development is not a new concept. The eighteenth-century Saxon forestry and mining official von Carlowitz (1713) might have invented sustainability. Timber scarcity in Europe made him seek 'equality' between reforestation/forest growth and harvesting of timber so as to ensure a 'continuous, persistent and sustained utilization' (von Carlowitz 1713: 105–6; author's translation). Over two and a half centuries later, the World Conservation Strategy called for 'sustainable development' by means of conserving our living resources (IUCN *et al.* 1980). Essentially the Strategy caters to ecological principles of maintaining the carrying capacities of ecosystems (Chapter 3). To link carrying capacity and resilience of nature to development, and hence its sustainability, ecological economists suggest safe minimum standards (Chapter 4) that could curb economic activity (Opschoor and van der Straaten 1993; Rennings *et al.* 1999; Ekins *et al.* 2003). The Earth Summits of the United Nations (Chapter 10) appear to adopt the broad definition of the World Commission on Environment and Development (WCED 1987). The 2002 Summit called for 'the integration of the three components of sustainable development – economic development, social development and environmental protection – as interdependent and mutually reinforcing pillars' (United Nations 2003: 12).

Development indices are mostly averages of standardized (to obtain a common scale) indicators. Normally, they give equal weight to the underlying indicators, irrespective of their role and significance in development:

- The Sustainable Development Index (SDI) averages 58 statistical measures in economic, environmental, social, demographic and political areas (Nováček and Mederly 2002).
- The Human Development Index (HDI) is an average of life expectancy, education (mean and expected years of schooling) and gross national income per capita (UNDP 2010).
- The Well-Being Index is an average of 81 indicators of human and ecosystem well-being; the assumption is that sustainable development is a combination of the two well-being categories of human needs satisfaction and life support of ecosystems (Prescott-Allen 2001).
- The Environmental Sustainability Index (ESI) calculates the mean of 68 measures of environmental stress, health effects, and the capacity to attain sustainable development (Yale Center for Environmental Law and Policy and Center for International Earth Science Information Network 1997–2006).

A comparison of the HDI, which excludes environmental concerns, with the SDI reveals high correlation of the indices (Bartelmus 2008). Reviewing eleven indices, Böhringer and Jochem (2007: 1) find them all 'useless if not misleading with respect to concrete policy advice'.

The **World Trade Organization** (WTO) was designed to foster trade liberalization. The Marrakesh Agreement establishing the WTO subscribes to 'sustainable development, seeking both to protect and preserve the environment and to enhance the means for doing so' (WTO n.d.(c)). Various WTO articles also specify exemptions from free trade rules. In particular, GATT Article 20, carried forward by the WTO, calls for 'protecting human, animal and plant life or health'. Environmentalists still complain about the lack of transparency and accountability of the WTO. Speth (2003) criticizes the narrow focus of the WTO on the effects of environmental policy on trade to the neglect of the effects of trade on the environment. The WTO website provides detailed descriptions of its environmental policy (from the WTO's point of view) (WTO n.d.(b)). The site also describes the current state of the – some will say 'moribund' – Doha negotiations on environment and development (WTO n.d.(a)).

Globalization can be defined as a process of rapidly increasing integration of lifestyles, markets and the production of goods and services across national boundaries. It has been facilitated by new information and transportation technologies and trade liberalization. Environmentalists stress the negative effects of globalization, and especially a power shift from governments to transnational corporations (Daly 1999; Mander 2003). Economists argue 'in defense' of corporations and globalization (Bhagwati 2002, 2004). Rodrik (1997) gives a concise and more neutral assessment of the effects of globalization. International organizations see information and communication technologies as a key driver of global development (Chapter 7).

Points for discussion

- What are the goals of sustainable development? Are they happiness and human welfare (as stipulated by the US Declaration of Independence and its Constitution)? Or meeting the human needs of the popular WCED definition of sustainable development?
- The 2010 summit conference on the Millennium Development Goals saw progress in some goals, but mostly failure in attaining environmental sustainability. Do we have a real commitment to meet the goals by 2015?
- Can we equate economic development with economic growth, and sustainability with environmental protection? Do governments do so?
- What do the indicators and indices of sustainable development tell us? Do they give us an operational definition of sustainable development?
- Globalization is blamed for inequities in the international and intergenerational distribution of environmental and economic goods and services. Do you agree?
- Should 'greens love trade', as argued by *The Economist* (9 October 1999)?
- Why do ecological economists embrace sustainable development?
- One reviewer of this book found the chapters on sustainable development rather vague. Do you agree? Whose fault is it – the author's or the paradigm's inherent opacity?

10 What should we do about it?

- *Local eco-development* has had some success but cannot replace national policies of sustainable development
- *Governments* subscribe to sustainable development but focus on economic growth in practice
- Earth Summits and international conventions show little clout in *global governance* for sustainable development
- *Deglobalization* seeks to mitigate the negative effects of globalization
- *Greening the World Trade Organization* could reduce environmental impacts of trade liberalization
- *Has sustainable development run its course?* Probably, as far as concrete policy advice is concerned

Sustainable development calls for **integrated policies** to deal with trade-offs and synergisms among its objectives. For example, farming bio-fuels may revive agrarian economies and reduce the use of fossil fuels and their emissions; it could also impair food security by crowding out food crops. One can hardly take issue with considering all pillars of sustainable development, especially when the paradigm remains in the lofty heights of 'transdisciplinary' philosophy (e.g. Lawn 2007: 3). Dissent sets in, however, when the paradigm faces the priorities and policies of the different disciplines behind its pillars. As discussed, opposing worldviews about the role and significance of nature for human welfare are the reason for the polarization of environmentalists and economists (Chapters 1, 8, 9). Reaching consensus depends, however, not only on interdisciplinary disputes but also on *where* decisions are taken. Figure 10.1 raises the question whether first responses to environmental problems should be local, national or global.

At the **local** – community – **level**, the closeness of people to each other and nature could facilitate agreement on social, cultural, ecological and

Figure 10.1 Think globally and act locally? Why not the other way round? Thinking about and assessing local impacts in countries could trigger global action. The popular slogan is probably moot since we need assessment and action at all levels.

economic conditions and their management. Agrarian communities, in particular, are tied to, and more knowledgeable about, the rhythm and use of nature than policy-makers in distant capitals. This would make the case for applying the resilience and carrying capacity concepts of ecological sustainability at the local level (Chapter 2). And indeed, in the 1970s, the United Nations Environment Programme launched eco-development as local-level development, which 'respect[s] the natural ecosystems and local sociocultural patterns' (UNEP 1975). Later case studies focused on the participation of the local population, unconventional eco-techniques and environmental education (Sachs 1976, 1980). Figure 10.2 shows some examples of traditional and novel technologies that have successfully been applied in local development.

Eco-development sank into oblivion until the Rio Earth Summit revived parts of it under its local Agenda 21 programmes (United Nations 1994).

Rice terraces, Philippines
keralaarticles.com/.../
banau-rice-terraces.jpg

Fish farming, Madagascar
www.proparco.fr/... /
Aqualma.jpg

Ethanol fuel, Brazil
Mariordo Mario Roberto Duran Orti

Drip irrigation, New Mexico
http://photogallery.
nrcs.usda.gov/Index.asp

Traditional housing, Lesotho
Nicholas DeVore—
Stone/Getty Images

Traditional medicine, China
User: Vbergera

Figure 10.2 Eco-techniques: at the heart of eco-development as advanced by the United Nations Environment Programme. They include diverse approaches to ecosystem management such as biological pest control, aquaculture, renewable energy sources, eco-dwelling and traditional medicine.

Local governmental programmes and grassroots movements met with limited success, though, due to lack of funds and resistance from powerful elites and central government.* To date, there is no surge of local initiatives, as some opponents of globalization would have it (Mander 2001).

So what can we expect from **national policies,** which face a much greater variety of opinions and preferences than close-knit agrarian communities? Figure 10.3 reveals that even the environment-friendly Dutch rank environmental issues below other high-priority social concerns. Note also that for the first time in the history of Gallup polls recession-shocked US Americans gave (in March 2009) higher priority to economic growth than to environmental protection (Newport 2009).

The question is to what extent volatile public opinion does and should influence governmental priorities and policies. Germany is often seen as a role model for sustainable development – at least for its efforts on climate change and renewable energy. The government's 2008 progress report *For a Sustainable Germany* (Federal Government 2008) elevated sustainable development from an assessment by an environmental agency to a guideline for the whole government under the direct patronage of the chancellor. Non-governmental organizations produced their own sustainability report

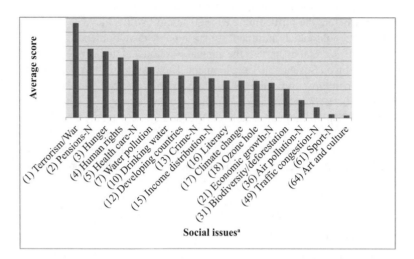

Figure 10.3 Priorities for sustainable development, the Netherlands. A sample survey by the Dutch environmental authorities measured the average score that citizens gave to 64 topics of a social agenda for sustainability. Note the relatively low ranking of most environmental concerns. Climate change issues come in at rank 17, comparable to the rating of economic growth (21). Are environmentalists and economists out of step with society's priorities?

Source: Netherlands Environmental Assessment Agency (2007), with permission from the Netherlands Environment Assessment Agency.

Note: [a]World-wide concern, except where marked 'N' – for the Netherlands only.

at the same time. Their rejection of the government's continuing focus on sustainable economic growth* does not augur well for public–private partnership, promoted by the World Summit on Sustainable Development (United Nations 2003). In fact, such alliance of governments and unelected groups of corporations, trade unions and civil society could be seen as shirking governmental responsibility for long-term socio-economic and environmental policy.

Poverty in developing countries and cross-border and global environmental impacts justify shifting some responsibility for implementing sustainable development to international organizations. As the German government puts it: 'The goals of sustainability cannot be achieved through national efforts alone' (Federal Government 2008: 203). The real motive of showing 'global responsibility' (Federal Government 2008: 162) might be fear of surging immigration and conflicts about access to natural resources. **Global governance** for sustainable development is anaemic, though. The Earth Summits in Stockholm and Rio de Janeiro were a good start, but the latest summit in Johannesburg did not live up to expectations. It remains to be seen whether the forthcoming Rio+20 summit will achieve its objectives of renewed political commitment for sustainable development.*

A small secretariat serves the annual sessions of the United Nations Commission on Sustainable Development. The Commission was established in order to follow up on the 1992 Rio Summit's Action Plan, Agenda 21 (Figure 10.4); it also provides 'policy guidance' on the Johannesburg Summit's Plan of Implementation (of Agenda 21). Leaving the global implementation of sustainable development to a relatively weak international organ indicates that a reductionist mode (Figure 9.1) prevails also at the international level. Strengthening the United Nations Environment Programme and

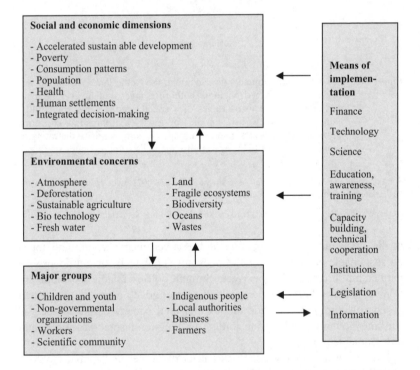

Figure 10.4 Agenda 21. The Rio Summit's programme of action for sustainable development calls for the integration of environment and development in its first block of social and economic dimensions. Environmental concerns cover the strategies for environmental protection and conservation. Public participation and global partnership are the goals for the major groups of civil society. The means of implementation comprise the policy instruments discussed in Chapter 7.

Source: Bartelmus (1994: 146, Figure 6.1), with permission from Taylor & Francis.

its small environmental fund of about US$170 million has been the mantra of UNEP's Governing Council. Some call, therefore, for a 'World Environment Organization' (Simonis 2005) with similar powers of monitoring, arbitration and sanctions as the World Trade Organization.

Globalization has generated interdependencies of economy, environment, culture and social justice across borders. Lack of data and uncertainty about the future of globalization and its impacts prevent a conclusive assessment of the sustainability effects of globalization (Chapter 9). The recent financial crisis of industrialized countries might slow globalization or change its direction towards increased South–South trading and cooperation. Also, European socially restrained capitalism now looks like a better model for trade and development than American free-for-all capitalism. Still, in one form or other we can expect globalization to continue. Depending on whether one sees globalization as inevitable or as the result of the unfettered greed of transnational corporations one would take radically different action:

- Most environmentalists consider globalization as reversible; they would therefore counter globalization by local-level development and by reining in or even dismantling the World Trade Organization.
- Economists see the positive effects of globalization-triggered economic growth; their objective is to change only those features of globalization that generate the worst side effects.

Localization is the most radical proposal for undoing globalization. To empower local government and non-governmental institutions is to counteract and ultimately replace globalization by a 'new set of international agreements that operate from an entirely different noncorporate hierarchy of values' (Mander 2003: 128). Effective local decision-making would, however, require a highly unlikely transfer of central powers to local institutions. Non-governmental organizations also lack democratic legitimization for implementing national policy concerns. Moreover, deglobalization could set off protectionist trade policies that could decrease economic growth and standards of living in many countries (Figure 10.5). For environmentalists this is not necessarily an unwelcome effect if it benefits the environmental cause.

Curbing the power of or changing the rules governing globalization's protagonist, the **World Trade Organization** (Chapter 9), could change the nature of globalization without rejecting it. Suggestions range from waiving WTO trade rules for environmental protection to participation of environmental organizations in WTO boards and conferences. Such greening of the WTO might, however, invite protectionist trade restrictions under the cloak

Figure 10.5 Deglobalization. Reintroducing protectionist tariffs and trade control at national borders could restrain economic growth, as well as its environmental impacts. It could also decrease standards of living.

of environmental protection. A more balanced approach would be to create countervailing environmental power by strengthening international organizations, notably the United Nations Environment Programme. Another option could give more bite to multilateral environmental agreements (MEAs) such as those dealing with trade in endangered species, hazardous wastes or ozone-depleting substances. It remains to be seen whether the sluggish Doha negotiations (Chapter 9) will come to some agreement on WTO and MEA rules.

The international community seems to have settled at present for soliciting the goodwill of global governmental and non-governmental players. The idea is to foster social and environmental responsibility and partnership in a **Global Compact** of stake- and shareholders (Figure 10.6).* The question is whether international proclamations will remain mostly rhetoric. Note that the repeatedly modified Development Decades returned in the end to economic growth as initially advocated, and the international commitment to the Millennium Development Goals remains questionable (Chapter 9).

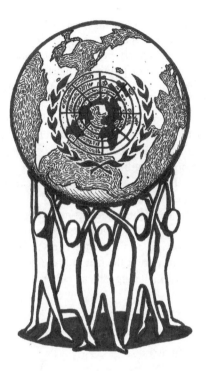

Figure 10.6 Global Compact: ideal, strategy or rhetoric?

Measurement problems, normative features, and lack of a common theory and policy throw **sustainable development** into question. Its advocates fail to explain why all social concerns and policies should be pressed into one ill-defined notion and an unwieldy policy framework. Such compression might actually obscure important issues and objectives, encourage inaction and open the door to hidden agendas. Nonetheless, ecological economists and like-minded environmentalists have attempted to upgrade sustainable development. A new field of 'sustainability science' should address the 'interactions between nature and society' (Kates *et al.* 2001: 641). These attempts are not convincing. Broad calls for networking, fund raising and advocacy look more like an activist agenda pursuing a lofty ideal than a new scientific approach to sustaining environment and development.

Integrative assessments and policies should probably focus on what can be reasonably well defined, measured and compared. We saw that this is the case for the economic (and to some extent also ecological) sustainability of economic performance and growth (Chapters 4, 7 and 8). Fact-based sustainability economics and its operational economic sustainability concept

(Chapter 6) come closer to a 'science' than sustainable development, at least inasmuch as one can consider economics as a science. Ecological economics does handle issues of natural sciences, notably of ecology, but its sustainability concepts fail to adequately integrate economic activity (Chapters 2 and 8). Most social, cultural or political concerns are difficult to quantify and compare; they need to be left to the national and international agencies designed for their implementation, rather than being mixed up under an opaque paradigm. Interdepartmental coordination and cooperation should handle, at least for now, the trade-offs and synergisms of economic-environmental with other societal objectives.

Sustainable development still holds considerable social and environmental goodwill. It also draws attention to prerequisites for economic growth and development such as peace, security and institutional support. Loud calls for the demise of the paradigm might harm the acceptance and pursuit of social and environmental goals. So, has sustainable development run its course? Probably, in so far as it can give concrete policy advice. Probably not, when considering the need to remind policy-makers of less tangible goals of society, including ethical, cultural and aesthetic aspects of the environment.

Want to know more?

One reason for the weak role of **eco-development** in implementing sustainable development is the large variety of local conditions, cultures and priorities, which have stymied the search for a general theory or model. Fostering a **local Agenda 21** by top-down (governmental) prompting and support also has achieved little. A survey of local Agenda 21 initiatives by an international association of local governments (United Nations Department of Economic and Social Affairs 2002) showed that cash-strapped municipalities mostly boasted improved water supply. In developing countries, bottom-up (grassroots) local initiatives have frequently met with the resistance of central and regional governments fearing the loss of power to local movements. Even where local development efforts have succeeded, corporations and local elites are known to plunder the fruits of development (Martinez-Alier 2002).

Germany's sustainability report is available on the government's website (Federal Government 2008). Targeted indicators are to monitor implementation, covering 21 social, economic and environmental themes. As it happened, a coalition of non-governmental organizations produced their own assessment of Germany's sustainability at the same time (BUND *et al.* 2008). Their report rejects the government's objective of balancing all dimensions of sustainability as 'assimilation and domestication' (BUND *et al.* 2008: 17; author's translation) of sustainable development. In their view, Germany needs a fundamental policy change, which uses governmental authority 'to push back the dominance of capital interests' in favour of the 'interests of nature and people' (BUND *et al.* 2008: 607; author's translation).

A series of **Earth Summits** has kept alive the debate of environment and development and their sustainability. The environmental movement and its dire predictions triggered the first *United Nations Conference on the Human Environment* (1972) in Stockholm. The Conference found that both the lack of development ('pollution of poverty') and gain of prosperity ('pollution of affluence') cause environmental problems. The Conference called, therefore, for the environmental dimension to be integrated into national and international development strategies. It also established the United Nations Environment Programme to implement and monitor an Action Plan for the Human Environment.

Responding to persistent policy failure on environment and development (Chapter 9), the World Commission on Environment and Development recommended that a UN Programme of Action on Sustainable Development be set up, promoted by an international conference (WCED 1987). In 1992, the *United Nations Conference on Environment and Development* convened in Rio de Janeiro (United Nations 1994). It adopted sustainable development and translated the paradigm into an international action programme, Agenda 21, a Rio Declaration and conventions, including the Framework Convention on Climate Change (UNFCCC n.d.).

A progress review of the Rio Summit, Rio+5, found a lethargic response to the Agenda 21 recommendations, reflected in the meagre flows of promised financial aid (Osborn and Bigg 1998). The 2002 *World Summit on Sustainable Development* in Johannesburg (United Nations 2003) did not break the lethargy, despite an attempt to include civil society through 'public–private partnership' (United Nations 2003: 48). Progress and achievements of the forthcoming *2012 Rio+20 Earth Summit* are discussed on the official website of the conference

(United Nations 2011b) and, more critically, by non-governmental stakeholders (Stakeholder Forum on a Sustainable Future, n.d.).

In 2000 the Secretary-General of the United Nations launched the **Global Compact** between international organizations, business and civil society (United Nations 2011a). The Compact thus anticipated the goal of public–private partnership proclaimed at the 2002 Johannesburg Summit. The objective is to solicit support from corporations and civil society for sustainability principles and the Millennium Development Goals (Chapter 9). The ten principles of the Compact include standards for human rights, labour, environmental protection and anti-corruption. To date, over 8,700 corporations and stakeholder organizations in more than 130 countries have signed up.

Points for discussion

- Is sustainable development a fig leaf behind which governments hide their real objectives of maximizing economic growth and employment?
- Where is the best place for implementing sustainable development? What can be done at local, national or international levels?
- Can local eco-development contribute to national sustainable development?
- Should we curb the power of the World Trade Organization by, for example, creating a countervailing World Environment Organization?
- What is the role of civil society in spurring sustainable development? Should governments transfer some of their social and environmental policies to (unelected) non-governmental organizations?
- Is sustainable development more than a wish list for social progress or welfare? Can it provide a framework for attaining all societal goals?
- Are Earth Summits useful tools for promoting sustainable development? What do you expect from the 2012 Summit? What are its results (if you read this after the Summit)?
- Has sustainable development run its course?

11 Some conclusions

What is countable?
What counts? What should
we do about it?

- *Micro- and macro-concepts* of ecological, economic and development sustainability
- Integrated environmental-economic accounts provide *operational indicators of sustainable economic growth*
- *Economic sustainability* is a necessary but not sufficient condition for sustaining economic growth
- *Technology* might save us from non-sustainability but is hard to predict
- *Market instruments* are efficient and less intrusive policy tools, but *rules and regulations* can be more effective
- *Non-countables* of sustainable development *count*, but are prone to political manipulation
- *Coordination* of sustainable economic growth with other concerns of sustainable development has to be *left to politics*
- *Sustainability economics* defines benchmarks for sustaining the economy and the environment

---

Participants at an international meeting on business and sustainability (Goodenough College, London, 12–13 June 2009) pronounced the concept of sustainability redundant. Why focus on the status quo, they asked, when the actual objective is to increase welfare? Moreover, available data systems and models can handle the interaction of economy and environment without resorting to an obscure concept. These arguments may come as no surprise in times of economic crisis when corporate social responsibility (Chapter 4) may have weakened. But then international organizations, governments and environmentalists still adhere to sustainable development (Chapters 9, 10).

For some overall conclusions let us return to the meaning and measurability of sustainability, and find out what it can do for us and what we can do about it. The three parts of this book describe three different **categories of sustainability** (Figure 11.1):

- ecological sustainability of the resilience of ecosystems and the carrying capacity of territories (Chapter 3);
- economic sustainability of welfare or economic growth, accounting for environmental damage or produced and natural capital consumption (Chapter 6);
- sustainability of development, which seeks to meet the needs of society now and in the future (Chapter 9).

We also found that ecological economics focuses on the physical base of the environment–economy interaction. It tends, therefore, to downplay economic sustainability and its monetary valuations; instead it suggests standards and regulations for determining and implementing biophysical ecological sustainability. In contrast, environmental economics and economic sustainability seek to integrate environmental impacts in monetary economic analysis; environmental economics may, however, use some of the standards of ecological sustainability for measuring and modelling environmental damage and maintenance costs. Market instruments are the preferred policy tool. Advocates of sustainable development do not usually distinguish between economic and ecological sustainability; they would probably subsume both categories under the economic and environmental pillars of the paradigm.

All sustainability categories refer to **micro** (including local) **and macro levels of analysis**. Table 11.1 shows the resilience of ecosystems to perturbations as local-level ecological sustainability, whereas carrying capacity refers usually to people and their activities in larger regions, countries or the planet.

Figure 11.1 Sustainability categories. (A) Ecological sustainability maintains ecosystems and carrying capacities of nature. (B) Economic sustainability maintains economic activity and its outputs, accounting for the cost of environmental depletion and degradation. (C) Sustainable development seeks to meet the needs and aspirations of the present and future generations.

Table 11.1 Micro- and macro-concepts of sustainability

Sustainability categories	Micro and local levels	Macro level
Ecological sustainability	Resilience of local ecosystems	Maintenance of carrying capacities of territories
Economic sustainability of well-being and welfare	Non-declining utility, allowing for disutility from environmental damage	Non-declining welfare, allowing for welfare losses from environmental damage
Economic sustainability of capital maintenance	Produced and natural capital maintenance for sustaining the productivity of enterprises	Produced and natural capital maintenance for sustaining economic growth
Sustainable development	Sustaining local communities through bottom-up eco-development	Sustaining society now and in the future through top-down policies

Economic sustainability sets out from micro-economic well-being (utility) of individuals and defines non-declining macro-economic welfare as a rather abstract sustainability concept. Alternatively, integrated economic-environmental accounts define a more practical economic sustainability concept as produced and natural capital maintenance. The purpose is to sustain income and output of enterprises, economic sectors and the national economy. Sustainable development encompasses all human needs and aspirations at local, national and international levels.

So **what is measurable?** The hardly quantifiable notion of utility disqualifies non-declining welfare as an operational measure of economic sustainability (Chapters 5 and 6). The ecological concept of the carrying capacity of a territory depends on the widely differing resiliences of ecosystems and desirable living standards of a territory's inhabitants. In practice, ecological sustainability applies most usefully to the management of local ecosystems, rather than larger regions (Chapter 3). Proxy measures of national or global ecological sustainability, like the Ecological Footprint and Total Material Requirement, suffer from questionable conversions of environmental impacts into area and weight equivalents (Chapter 3). Finally, the broad concept of sustainable development does not gain credibility by aggregating large numbers of mostly incomparable economic, social and environmental indicators (Chapter 9). For applied analysis and policy, this leaves us with economic sustainability of capital maintenance for sustaining economic output and consumption. Some international organizations seem now to have reached similar conclusions, calling for a 'green economy'

(UNEP 2011b) or 'green economic growth' (OECD 2011); however, they still see the greening of economic activity as part of a broader strategy of sustainable development.

To assess economic sustainability integrated environmental-economic accounts use monetary values. Expanded market values reflect, at least in principle, individual preferences for environmental and economic goods and services. The accounts deduct the costs of produced and natural capital consumption from the value of output and capital formation as measures of net economic performance and sustainable economic growth (Chapter 6).

The first conclusion is that **integrated environmental-economic accounting is the only way to obtain operational measures of the sustainability of both economy and environment**. The accounts define and measure the necessary conditions for sustaining economic performance and growth as the maintenance of produced and natural capital.

One should not overlook, however, that environmentally adjusted economic indicators ignore the maintenance of human, social and institutional capital. For these less tangible types of capital we lack compatible accounting concepts and measures. Also, accounting for the total value of produced and natural capital reflects weak sustainability, which assumes substitutability of different production factors (Chapter 6). Strong ecological sustainability calls for the preservation of non-substitutable critical natural capital (Chapter 3); this is the objective of ecological economics. Whether we can replace critical natural capital by reproducible production factors depends on technological progress (Chapter 7).

The second conclusion is that **economic sustainability will improve but not necessarily ensure the overall sustainability of economic performance and growth**. Strong ecological sustainability reminds us that economic activity could face potentially critical environmental constraints. Technological progress might be the saviour but is difficult to predict.

Introducing physical environmental limits into economic analysis could be the way to overcome the persistent dichotomy between ecological and environmental economics and their strong and weak sustainability notions. Introducing normative ecological standards into positivist economic analysis may clarify the relationships between the two disciplines and could reveal judgemental assumptions in modelling. Mixing norms with facts, however, blurs the 'scientific' analysis of the environment–economy interface (Chapters 8 and 10).

The third conclusion is that **introducing ecological norms and standards into economic analysis can provide alternative policy scenarios for optional environmental targets**, but at the risk of manipulating the sustainability picture by judgement and advocacy.

The next conclusion could be to discard all non-operational (non-quantifiable) sustainability concepts, following the World Bank's (2003b: 15) assertion that 'people value what they measure'. This view belittles the importance of intangible values such as knowledge, culture or altruism. Selecting and targeting indicators for the wide range of rather generic sustainable development goals may be judgemental, but makes the vision of sustainable development more visible (Chapters 2 and 9). The questions remain: what does greater visibility reveal – in other words, what do the indicators and their targets tell us about their significance in attaining sustainability?

The fourth conclusion is that **non-countables count, but we do not know how much**. All one can do is to signal their relevance – rather than significance – by using indicators and their targets for measuring particular target compliance or violation.

What should we do about it? The evaluation of sustainability by sets of selected indicators and indicator averages is judgemental; so is enforcing environmental targets and standards by rules and regulations. In contrast, market valuation in environmental accounts gives us observable or at least reproducible cost measures of attaining sustainability. One can use these costs to change the environmentally damaging behaviour of households and enterprises by means of market instruments. At the macro-economic level, (re)investment policy can offset produced and natural capital loss in so far as these capitals can be restored or substituted. Where these policies do not work, either because of the loss of critical natural capital or delays and inefficiencies in implementation, harder tools of command and control would have to supplement market instruments (Chapter 7).

The fifth conclusion is that **environmental-cost-based market instruments and investments are less invasive** and less judgemental tools of attaining weak economic sustainability. **Rules and regulations impose the collective will** when individual preferences are unable or unwilling to account for critical environmental impacts.

The aggregation problem looms large in attempts at integrating socioeconomic and environmental policies of sustainable growth and development. Combining *all* policies in one planning and budgeting framework is bound to mislead when the contributions of different policies to a hazy goal remain in the dark. Achieving cornucopian sustainable development is an illusion, except perhaps for local eco-development (Chapter 10). We have no unequivocal definition of sustainable development, nor a blueprint for its implementation. Still, goodwill attached to the paradigm may help advocate and drive acceptance of environmental and social policies. Priorities for and coordination of the wide range of national and international development policies have to be settled through political negotiation.

The sixth conclusion is: **rational policies can tackle fact-based sustainable economic growth; coordination with other development concerns has to be left to politics.**

So, what can sustainability economics do for us? Obviously, it cannot solve all environmental and economic problems, but it can tell us where integrated environmental and economic policies:

- face uncertainty when lack of facts and figures blurs the assessment of economic performance and environmental impacts (Chapters 2 and 3);
- become normative and judgemental when using ecological sustainability standards and rules for securing nature's life support (Chapter 4);
- turn opaque when drowned in cornucopian notions of human well-being, quality of life or sustainable development (Chapters 5 and 9); and
- work best when quantifiable benchmarks of economic sustainability indicate when and where produced and natural capital need to be replaced (Chapters 6 and 7); the purpose is to avoid a decline of output, income and consumption, in other words, to sustain economic growth.

All in all, we seem to know less than we believe, and to believe more than we believe. Sustainability economics helps to pin down facts and figures as opposed to convictions and advocacy in the charged debate of the sustainability or non-sustainability of our economies. Introducing environmental constraints into economic sustainability analysis shows the way towards a common operational theory of sustainability economics (Chapter 8).

The seventh conclusion is: **sustainability economics assesses the sustainability of the economy and generates benchmarks for prudent environmental and economic behaviour and policies**. A practical framework for integrative environmental and economic analysis and policy could be its next achievement.

Points for discussion

- Why should we be content with sustaining the environment and economic performance when we could improve them?
- Market instruments versus command and control: what is more important for attaining sustainability – efficiency or efficacy?
- What is measurable is manageable. What about intangibles such as aesthetic and ethical aspects of the environment? Should we leave them to individual convictions and behaviour, or to the collective will of governments?
- How do intangibles (non-countables) enter the sustainability equation? What can economics do about it?
- 'What's economics got to do with it?' we asked in Chapter 1. Can we be more specific now, after exploring the three sustainability categories?
- Is sustainability economics a new discipline in its own right?
- What next? Look for unresolved and controversial issues and draw up your own agenda for research and policy.

References

AAG Center for Global Geography Education (2011) 'Population and natural resources module: conceptual framework'. <http://globalgeography.aag.org/ PopulationandNaturalResources1e/CF_PopNatRes_Jan10/CF_PopNatRes_ Jan1011.html> (accessed 18 June 2011).

Arrow, K., Dasgupta, P., Goulder, L., Daily, G., Ehrlich, P., Heal, G, Levin, S., Karl-Mäter, G., Schneider, S., Starrett, D. and Walker, B. (2004) 'Are we consuming too much?', *Journal of Economic Perspectives*, 18: 147–72.

Arrow, K.J., Dasgupta, P. and Mäler, K.-G. (2003) 'Evaluating projects and assessing sustainable development in imperfect economies', *Environmental and Resource Economics*, 26: 647–85.

Atkinson, G., Dietz, S. and Neumayer, E. (eds) (2007) *Handbook of Sustainable Development*, Cheltenham: Edward Elgar.

Auty, R.M. (1993) *Sustaining Development in Mineral Economies: the Resource Curse Thesis*, London: Routledge.

Ayres, R.U. and Ayres, L.W. (eds) (2002) *A Handbook of Industrial Ecology*, Cheltenham: Edward Elgar.

Barbier, E.B. (1997) 'Introduction to the environmental Kuznets curve, special issue', *Environment and Development Economics*, 2: 357–81.

Bartelmus, P. (1979) 'Limits to development – environmental constraints of human needs satisfaction', *Journal of Environmental Management*, 9: 255–69.

—— (1994) *Environment, Growth and Development, the Concepts and Strategies of Sustainability*, London: Routledge.

—— (2001) 'Accounting for sustainability: greening the national accounts', in M.K. Tolba (ed.) (2001) *Our Fragile World, Challenges and Opportunities for Sustainable Development*, Oxford: Eolss Publishers.

—— (2002) 'Unveiling wealth – accounting for sustainability', in P. Bartelmus (ed.) *Unveiling Wealth, On Money, Quality of Life and Sustainability*, Dordrecht: Kluwer.

—— (2004) 'Green accounting and energy', in C. Cleveland (ed.) *Encyclopedia of Energy*, ElsevierScience. <http://www.sciencedirect.com/science/referenceworks/ 012176480X> (accessed 18 July 2011).

——— (2008) *Quantitative* Eco-*nomics, How Sustainable Are Our Economies?*, Dordrecht: Springer.

——— (2009) 'The cost of natural capital consumption: accounting for a sustainable world economy', *Ecological Economics*, 68: 1850–7.

Bartelmus, P. and Seifert, E.K. (eds) (2003) *Green Accounting*, Aldershot: Ashgate.

Bartelmus, P., Stahmer, C. and van Tongeren, J. (1991) 'Integrated environmental and economic accounting: Framework for a SNA satellite system', *Review of Income and Wealth*, 37: 111–48.

Beckerman, W. (1992) 'Economic growth and the environment: whose growth? Whose environment?', *World Development*, 20: 481–96.

——— (1994) 'Sustainable development: is it a useful concept?', *Environmental Values*, 3: 191–209.

Bhagwati, J. (2002) 'Coping with antiglobalization', *Foreign Affairs*, 81: 2–7.

——— (2004) *In Defense of Globalization*, New York: Oxford University Press.

Biomimicry Institute (2007–2011) 'What is biomimicry?'. <http://www.biomimicryinstitute.org/about-us/what-is-biomimicry.html> (accessed 3 July 2011).

Bishop, R.C. (1978) 'Endangered species and uncertainty: the economics of a safe minimum standard', *American Journal of Agricultural Economics*, 30: 461–74.

Böhringer, C. and Jochem, P.E.P. (2007) 'Measuring the immeasurable – a survey of sustainability indices', *Ecological Economics*, 63: 1–8.

Brand, F. (2009) 'Critical natural capital revisited: ecological resilience and sustainable development', *Ecological Economics* 68: 605–12.

Bringezu, S. (1993) 'Towards increasing resource productivity: how to measure the total material consumption of regional or national economies?', *Fresenius Environmental Bulletin*, 2: 437–42.

——— (2002) 'Towards sustainable resource management in the European Union', *Wuppertal Papers* No. 121, Wuppertal, Germany: Wuppertal Institute for Climate, Environment and Energy.

Brown, L.R. (2006) *Plan B – Rescuing a Planet Under Stress and a Civilization in Trouble*, New York: Norton.

Brown, M.T. and Ulgiati, S. (1999) 'Emergy valuation of the biosphere and natural capital', *Ambio*, 28: 486–93.

BUND, EED and Brot für die Welt (eds) (2008) *Zukunftsfähiges Deutschland in einer globalisierten Welt* [Sustainable Germany in a globalized world], Frankfurt a.M.: Fischer.

Carnot, N.L.S. (1824/1966) *Réflexions sur la puissance motrice du feu et sur les machines propres à développer cette puissance* [Reflections on the motive power of fire and the machines appropriate for developing this power], London: Dawson.

Carson, R. (1965) *Silent Spring*, London: Penguin.

Castiglione, D., van Deht, J.W. and Wolleb, G. (eds) (2008) *The Handbook of Social Capital*, Oxford: Oxford University Press.

Centre for Bhutan Studies (2008) 'Gross national happiness'. <http://www.grossnationalhappiness.com/gnhIndex/gnhIndexVariables.aspx> (accessed 19 June 2011).

Ciriacy-Wantrup, S.V. (1952) *Resource Conservation: Economics and Policies*, Berkeley: University of California Press.

Clausius, R.J.E. (1850) 'Über die bewegende Kraft der Wärme' [On the moving force of heat], *Annalen der Physik*, 79: 368–97, 500–24.

Coastal Service Center, National Oceanic and Atmospheric Administration (NOAA) (n.d.) 'Restoration economics, irreversibility, sustainability and safe minimum standard'. <http://www.csc.noaa.gov/coastal/economics/irreversibility. htm> (accessed 19 July 2011).

Cobb, C., Halstead, T. and Rowe, J. (1995) 'If the GDP is up, why is America down?' *Atlantic Monthly*, October: 59–78.

Cole, H.S.D., Freeman, C., Jahoda, M. and Pavitt, K.L.R. (1973) *Models of Doom: A Critique of the Limits to Growth*, New York: Universe Books.

Commission of the European Communities (2005) *Thematic Strategy on the Sustainable Use of Natural Resources*, COM (2005) 670 final. <http://ec.europa. eu/environment/natres/> (accessed 19 July 2011).

Committee of Exports on Environmental Economic Accounting (2012) 'Revision of the System of Environmental-Economic Accounting (SEEA), central framework' (background document for the Statistical Commission at its 43rd session). <http://unstats.un.org/unsd/envaccounting/seearev/> (accessed 4 March 2012).

Conrad, K. (1999) 'Computable general equilibrium models for environmental economics and policy analysis', in J. van den Bergh (ed.) *Handbook of Environmental and Resource Economics*, Cheltenham: Edward Elgar.

Cortright, J. (2001) 'New growth theory, a practitioner's guide'. <http://www.eda. gov/ImageCache/EDAPublic/documents/pdfdocs/1g3lr_5f7_5fcortright_2epdf/ v1/1g3lr_5f7_5fcortright.pdf> (accessed 19 July 2011).

Costanza, R. (1980) 'Embodied energy and economic valuation', *Science*, 210: 1219–24.

Costanza, R., Daly, H.E. and Bartholomew, J.A. (1991) 'Goals, agenda and policy recommendations for ecological economics', in R. Costanza (ed.) *Ecological Economics, The Science and Management of Sustainability*, New York: Columbia University Press.

Costanza, R., Cumberland, J.H., Daly, H., Goodland R. and Norgaard, R.B. (1997a) *An Introduction to Ecological Economics*, Boca Raton, FL: St. Lucie Press.

Costanza, R., d'Arge, R., de Groot, R., Farber, S., Grass, M., Hannon, B., Limburg, K., Naeem, S., O'Neill, R.V., Paruelo, J., Raskin, R.G., Sutton, P. and van den Belt, M. (1997b) 'The value of the world's ecosystem services and natural capital', *Nature*, 387: 253–60.

Crook, C. (2005) 'The good company, a survey of corporate social responsibility', *The Economist*, 22 January 2005.

Crowards, T.M. (1996) 'Addressing uncertainty in project evaluation: the costs and benefits of safe minimum standards', CSERGE Working Paper GEC 96–04, University of East Anglia, UK. <http://www.uea.ac.uk/env/cserge/pub/wp/gec/ gec_1996_04.pdf> (accessed 19 July 2011).

Daly, H.E. (1990) 'Toward some operational principles of sustainable development', *Ecological Economics*, 2: 1–6.

—— (1996) *Beyond Growth*, Boston, MA.: Beacon Press.

—— (1999) 'Globalization versus internationalization – some implications', *Ecological Economics*, 3: 31–7.

—— (2005) 'Economics in a full world', *Scientific American* 293 (3): 100–7.

Daly, H.E. and Cobb, Jr., J.B. (1989) *For the Common Good: Redirecting the Economy Towards Community, the Environment, and a Sustainable Future*, Boston, MA.: Beacon Press.

Daly, H.E. and Farley, J. (2004) *Ecological Economics*, Washington, DC: Island Press.

Darwin, C. (1859/1951) *The Origin of Species*, New York: Dutton.

Dasgupta, P. (1994) 'Optimal versus sustainable development', in I. Serageldin and A. Steer (eds) *Valuing the Environment, Proceedings of the First Annual International Conference on Environmentally Sustainable Development*, Washington, DC: World Bank.

Dasgupta, P. and Mäler, K.-G. (1991) 'The environment and emerging development issues', in *Proceedings of the World Bank annual conference on development economics 1990*, Washington, DC: World Bank.

—— (2000) 'Net national product, wealth, and social well-being', *Environment and Development Economics*, 5: 69–93.

De Groot, R., van der Perk, J., Chiesura, A. and van Vliet, A. (2003) 'Importance and threat as determining factors of criticality of natural capital', *Ecological Economics*, 44: 187–204.

De Haan, M. and Kee, P. (n.d.) 'Accounting for sustainable development: the NAMEA-based approach'. Statistics Netherland. <http://www.cbs.nl/nr/rdonlyres/789fc43c-28ac-4a07-a4e1-158745589a50/0/accountingforsustainabledevelopmentthenameabasedapproach.pdf> (accessed 19 July 2011).

Diamond, J. (2005) *Collapse, How Societies Choose to Fail or Succeed*, London: Penguin Books.

Dixon, J.A., Fallon Scura, L., Carpenter, R.A. and Sherman, P.B. (1994) *Economic Analysis of Environmental Impacts*, London: Earthscan.

Dorfman, R., Samuelson, P.A. and Solow, R.M. (1958) *Linear Programming and Economic Analysis*, New York: McGraw-Hill.

Dziegielewska, D. 2009 'Total economic value', in *Encyclopedia of Earth*. <http://www.eoearth.org/article/Total_economic_value> (accessed 19 July 2011).

Ehrenfeld, J.R. and Chertow, M.R. (2002) 'Industrial symbiosis: the legacy of Kalundborg', in R.U. Ayres and L.W. Ayres (eds) *A Handbook of Industrial Ecology*, Cheltenham: Edward Elgar.

Ehrlich, P.R. and Holdren, J.P. (1971) 'Impact of population growth', *Science*, 171: 1212–17.

Ekins, P., Simon, S., Deutsch, L., Folke, C. and De Groot, R. (2003) 'A framework for the practical application of the concepts of critical natural capital and strong sustainability', *Ecological Economics*, 44: 165–85.

Ellerman, A.D. and Joskow, P.L. (2008) 'The European Union's trading system in perspective', paper prepared for the PEW Center on Global Climate Change. <http://www.pewclimate.org/eu-ets> (accessed 19 July 2011).

Elliot, R. (2001) 'Ethics and value', in M.K. Tolba (ed.) (2001) *Our Fragile World, Challenges and Opportunities for Sustainable Development*, Oxford: Eolss Publishers.

Elliot, S. (2007) 'Environmentally sustainable ICT: a critical topic for IS research?', Pacific Asia Conference of Information Systems, Proceedings. <http://aisel.aisnet.org/pacis2007/114/> (accessed 19 July 2011).

European Association for Bioeconomic Studies (EABS) (1997) *Implications and Applications of Bioeconomics*, Proceedings of the Second International Conference of the EABS (Palma de Mallorca, March 11–13, 1994), Milan: Edizioni Nagard.

European Commission (2007–2010) 'Beyond GDP'. <http://www.beyond-gdp.eu/> (accessed 19 June 2011).

European Commission, Enterprise and Industry (2011) 'Sustainable and responsible business, corporate social responsibility (CSR)'. http://ec.europa.eu/enterprise/policies/sustainable-business/corporate-social-responsibility/index_en.htm (accessed 26 July 2011).

European Commission, Environment (2011) 'EMAS'. <http://ec.europa.eu/environment/emas/index_en.htm> (accessed 19 June 2011).

European Commission, Information Society (n.d.) 'Digital agenda for Europe'. <http://ec.europa.eu/information_society/digital-agenda/index_en.htm> (accessed 19 June 2011).

European Commission, International Monetary Fund, Organisation for Economic Co-operation and Development, United Nations and World Bank (2009) *System of National Accounts 2008*, New York: United Nations (sales no. E.08.XVII.29). <http://unstats.un.org/unsd/nationalaccount/docs/SNA2008.pdf> (accessed 13 July 2011).

European Environment Agency (2002) *Benchmarking the Millennium*, Environmental Assessment Report No. 9, Luxembourg: Office for Official Publications of the European Communities. <http://www.eea.europa.eu/publications/environmental_assessment_report_2002_9> (accessed 18 June 2011).

—— (2005) 'EEA core set of indicators, guide', EEA Technical Report No. 1/2005. Luxembourg: Official Publications of the European Communities. <http://www.eea.europa.eu/publications/technical_report_2005_1> (accessed 18 June 2011).

—— (2010). *The European Environment – State and Outlook 2010, Synthesis*. Luxembourg: Office for Official Publications of the European Communities. <http://www.eea.europa.eu/soer/synthesis/synthesis/the-state-of-the-environment> (accessed 18 June 2011).

European Environment Agency (n.d.) 'What is an environmental indicator?'. <http://www.eea.europa.eu/help/eea-help-centre/faqs/what-is-an-environmental-indicator> (accessed 18 June 2011).

Eurostat (2001) *Economy-wide Material Flow Accounts and Derived Indicators: a Methodological Guide*, Luxembourg: European Communities.

Ewing, B., Moore, D., Goldfinger, S., Ourster, A., Leed, A. and Wackernagel, M. (2010) *Ecological Footprint Atlas 2010*, Oakland: Global Footprint Network. <http://www.footprintnetwork.org/images/uploads/Ecological_Footprint_Atlas_2010.pdf> (accessed 18 June 2011).

Faber, M., Petersen, T. and Schiller, J. (2002) 'Homo oeconomicus and homo politicus in ecological economics', *Ecological Economics*, 40: 323–33.

Factor 10 Club (1994) *Carnoules Declaration*, Wuppertal, Germany: Wuppertal Institute for Climate, Environment and Energy.

Faucheux, S. (2001) 'Summary principles for sustainable development', in M.K. Tolba (ed.) (2001) *Our Fragile World, Challenges and Opportunities for Sustainable Development*, Oxford: Eolss Publishers.

Federal Government (2008) *Progress Report 2008 on the National Strategy for Sustainable Development: For a Sustainable Germany*, Berlin: Press and Information Office of the Federal Government. <http://www.nachhaltigkeitsrat.de/fileadmin/user_upload/English/strategy/2008/German_Govt_NSDS_progress_report_08_E.pdf> (accessed 22 August 2011).

Frank, R.H. (1999) *Luxury Fever: Why Money Fails to Satisfy in an Era of Excess*, New York: Free Press.

Funtowicz, S.O. and Ravetz, J.R. (1991) 'A new scientific methodology for global environmental issues', in R. Costanza (ed.) *Ecological Economics: the Science and Management of Sustainability*, New York: Columbia University Press.

Gallup (2010) 'Americans less happy, more stressed in 2009'. <http://www.gallup.com/poll/124904/americans-less-happy-stressed-2009.aspx> (accessed 19 July 2011).

Georgescu-Roegen, N. (1971) *The Entropy Law and the Economic Process*, Cambridge, MA: Harvard University Press.

—— (1979) 'Energy analysis and economic valuation', *Southern Economic Journal*, 45: 1023–58.

Gore, A. (2006) *An Inconvenient Truth*, New York: Rodale.

Goulder, I.H. (1995) 'Environmental taxation and the double dividend, a reader's guide', *International Tax and Public Finance*, 2: 157–83.

Gray, R. and Bebbington, J. (2007) 'Corporate sustainability: accountability or impossible dream', in: G. Atkinson, S. Dietz and E. Neumayer (eds) (2007) *Handbook of Sustainable Development*, Cheltenham: Edward Elgar.

Grossman, G.M. and Krueger, A.B. (1995) 'Economic growth and the environment', *Quarterly Journal of Economics*, CX: 353–77.

Haeckel, E. (1866) *Generelle Morphologie der Organismen* [General morphology of organisms], vol. 2, Berlin: Reimer.

Hanley, N., Shogren, J.F. and White, B. (2007) *Environmental Economics in Theory and Practice*, 2nd edn, London: Palgrave Macmillan.

Hardin, G. (1968) 'The tragedy of the commons', *Science*, 162: 1243–48.

Hepburn, C. (2007) 'Valuing the far-off future: discounting and its alternatives', in: G. Atkinson, S. Dietz and E. Neumayer (eds) *Handbook of Sustainable Development*, Cheltenham, UK: Edward Elgar.

Hicks, J.R. (1939) *Value and Capital*, Oxford: Clarendon Press.

Hinterberger, F., Luks, F., Stewen, M. and van der Straaten J. (2000) 'Environmental policy in a complex world', *International Journal of Sustainable Development*, 3: 276–96.

Hoekstra, R. and van den Bergh, J.C.J.M. (2006) 'Constructing physical input–output tables for environmental modeling and accounting: framework and illustrations', *Ecological Economics*, 59: 375–93.

Holling, C.S. (ed.) (1978) *Adaptive Environmental Assessment and Management*, Chichester: Wiley.

Hotelling, H. (1931) 'The economics of exhaustible resources', *Journal of Political Economy*, 39: 137–75.

Huber, J. (2004) *New Technologies and Environmental Innovation*, Cheltenham: Edward Elgar.

Intergovernmental Panel on Climate Change (IPCC) (2007a) *Contribution of Working Group I to the Fourth Assessment Report of the IPCC: the Physical Base, Summary for Policy Makers*. <http://www.ipcc.ch/publications_and_data/ar4/wg1/en/contents.html> (accessed 19 July 2011).

—— (2007b) *Contribution of Working Group III to the Fourth Assessment Report of the IPCC: Mitigation of Climate Change, Summary for Policy Makers*. <http://www.ipcc.ch/publications_and_data/ar4/wg3/en/contents.html> (accessed 19 July 2011).

International Labour Organization (ILO) (1977) *Employment, Growth and Basic Needs: a One-world Problem*, New York: Praeger.

International Organization for Standardization (2011) 'ISO 14000 essentials'. <http://www.iso.org/iso/en/prods-services/otherpubs/iso14000/index.html> (accessed 19 June 2011).

IUCN (The World Conservation Union) (2006) *The Future of Sustainability, Re-thinking Environment and Development in the Twenty-first Century.* Report of the Renowned Thinkers Meeting, 29–31 January 2006. <http://cmsdata.iucn.org/downloads/iucn_future_of_sustainability.pdf> (accessed 24 August 2011).

International Union for Conservation of Nature and Natural Resources (IUCN), United Nations Environment Programme (UNEP) and World Wildlife Fund (WWF) (1980) *World Conservation Strategy, Living Resource Conservation for Sustainable Development*, Gland, Switzerland: IUCN.

Islam, S.M.N. (2001) 'Ecology and optimal economic growth: an optimal ecological economic growth model and its sustainability implications', in M. Munasinghe, O. Sunkel and C. de Miguel (eds) *The Sustainability of Long-term Growth: Socioeconomic and Ecological Perspectives*, Cheltenham: Edward Elgar.

Jevons, W.S. (1865/1965) *The Coal Question: an Inquiry Concerning the Progress of the Nation, and the Probable Exhaustion of Our Coal Mines*; reprint of the 3rd edn, New York: Augustus Kelly.

Kapp, K.W. (1950) *The Social Costs of Private Enterprise*, Boston, MA.: Harvard University Press.

Kates, R.W., Clark, W.C., Corell, R., Hall, J.M., Jaeger, C.C., Lowe, I., McCarthy, J.J., Schellnhuber, H.J., Bolin, B., Dickson, N.M., Faucheux, S., Gilberto, C., Gallopin, G.C., Grübler, A., Huntley, B., Jäger, J., Jodha, N.S., Kasperson, R.E., Mabogunje, A., Matson, P., Mooney, H., Moore III, B., O'Riordan, T. and Svedin, U. (2001) 'Sustainability science', *Science*, 292: 641–2.

Keynes, J.M. (1936/1973) *The General Theory of Employment, Interest and Money*, London: Macmillan.

Koopmans, T.C. (1973) 'Some observations on "optimal" economic growth and exhaustible resources', in H.C. Bos, H. Linnemann and P. de Wolff (eds) *Economic Structure and Development: Essays in Honour of Jan Tinbergen*, Amsterdam: North-Holland.

Krall, L. and Klitgaard, K. (2011) 'Ecological economics and institutional change', in R. Costanza, K. Limburg and I. Kubiszewski (eds) *Ecological Economics Reviews*, Annals of the New York Academy of Sciences, vol. 1219, New York: New York Academy of Sciences.

Kuznets, S. (1955) 'Economic growth and income inequality', *American Economic Review*, 45: 1–28.

Landefeld, J.S. and Howell, S.L. (1998) 'USA: integrated economic and environmental accounting: lessons from the IEESA', in K. Uno and P. Bartelmus (eds) *Environmental Accounting in Theory and Practice*, Dordrecht: Kluwer.

Lange, G.M. (2004) 'Wealth, natural capital and sustainable development: contrasting examples from Botswana and Namibia', *Environmental & Resource Economics'*, 29: 257–83.

Lawn, P. (2007) *Frontier Issues in Ecological Economics*, Cheltenham: Edward Elgar.

Leipert, C. (1989). 'National income and economic growth: the conceptual side of defensive expenditures', *Journal of Economic Issues*, 23: 843–56.

Leontief, W. (1951) *The Structure of American Economy 1919–1939, an Empirical Application of Equilibrium Analysis*, 2nd edn, New York: Oxford University Press.

—— (1970) 'Environmental repercussions and the economic structure: an input–output approach', *Review of Economics and Statistics*, 52: 262–71.

Levitt, S.D. and Dubner, S.J. (2005) *Freakonomics, the Hidden Side of Everything*, New York: Harper Perennial.

Lomborg, B. (2001) *The Skeptical Environmentalist, Measuring the Real State of the World*, Cambridge: Cambridge University Press.

Lotka, A.J. (1925/1956) *Elements of Physical Biology*, New York: Dover.

Lovelock, J.E. (1988/1995) *The Ages of Gaia – a Biography of Our Living Earth*, New York: Norton.

—— (2009) *The Vanishing Face of Gaia: A Final Warning*, New York: Basic Books.

McDonough, W. and Braungart, M. (2003) 'The cradle-to-cradle alternative'. <http://www.mcdonough.com/writings/cradle_to_cradle-alt.htm> (accessed 19 June 2011).

Malthus, T. (1798/1963) *Principles of Population*, Homewood, IL: R.D. Irwin.

Mander, J. (2001) 'Introduction: facing the rising tide', in E. Goldsmith and J. Mander (eds) *The Case Against the Global Economy and for a Turn Towards Localization*, London: Earthscan.

—— (2003) 'Intrinsic negative effects of economic globalization on the environment', in J.G. Speth (ed.) (2003) *Worlds Apart, Globalization and the Environment*, Washington, DC: Island Press.

Martinez-Alier, J. (2002) *The Environmentalism of the Poor, a Report for UNRISD for the WSSD*. <http://www.rcade.org/secciones/comisiones/comisiones/decol/jalier.PDF> (accessed 19 July 2011).

Marx, K. (1894/1991) *Capital, Vol. III* (ed. F. Engels, trans. D. Fernbach), Harmondsworth: Penguin.

Max-Neef, M. (1995) 'Economic growth and quality of life: a threshold hypothesis', *Ecological Economics*, 15: 115–118.

Max-Neef, M., Elizalde, A. and Hopenhayn, M. (1989) 'Human scale development: an option for the future', *Development Dialogue*, 1: 5–80.

Meadows, D.H., Meadows, D.L., Randers, J. and Behrens III, W.W. (1972) *The Limits to Growth*, New York: Universe Books.

Meadows, D.H., Meadows D.L. and Randers, J. (1992) *Beyond the Limits*, Post Mills, VT: Chelsea Green Publishing.

Meadows, D., Randers, J. and Meadows, D. (2004) *Limits to Growth, the 30-years Update*, White River Junction, VT: Chelsea Green Publishing.

Meyer, B. (1999) 'Research-statistical-policy co-operation in Germany: modelling with panta rhei', in European Commission (ed.) *From Research to Implementation: Policy-driven Methods for Evaluating Macro-economic Environmental Performance*, Luxembourg: European Communities.

———— (2005). 'The economic-environmental model Panta Rhei and its application', GWS Discussion Paper 2005/3. <http://www.gws-os.com/discussionpapers/gws-paper05- 3.pdf> (accessed 18 July 2011).

Millennium Ecosystem Assessment (2005) *Ecosystems and Human Well-being: Synthesis*, Washington, DC: Island Press. <http://www.maweb.org/documents/document.356.aspx.pdf> (accessed 19 July 2011).

Munasinghe, M. (ed.) (2002) *Macroeconomics and the Environment*, Cheltenham: Edward Elgar.

Murray, J. and Wood, R. (eds) (2010) *The Sustainability Practitioner's Guide to Input–output Analysis*, Champaign, IL: Common Ground.

Netherlands Environmental Assessment Agency (2007) 'How Dutch citizens prioritise the social agenda' (MNP Report 500086002/2007). <http://www.rivm.nl/bibliotheek/rapporten/500086002.pdf> (accessed 19 July 2011).

Newport, F. (2009) 'Americans: economy takes precedence over environment', Gallup. <http://www.gallup.com/poll/116962/Americans-Economy-Takes-Precedence-Environment.aspx> (accessed 19 July 2011).

Nordhaus, W.D. (1973) 'World dynamics: measurement without data', *Economic Journal*, 83: 1156–83.

———— (2008) *A Question of Balance, Weighing the Options on Global Warming Policies*, New Haven: Yale University Press.

Nordhaus, W.D. and Kokkelenberg, E.C. (eds) (1999) *Nature's Numbers – Expanding the National Accounts to Include the Environment*, Washington, DC: National Academy Press.

Nordhaus, W.D. and Tobin, J. (1973) 'Is growth obsolete?', *Studies in Income and Wealth*, 38: 509–64.

Norgaard, R.B. (1994) *Development Betrayed, the End of Progress and a Coevolutionary Revisioning of the Future*, London: Routledge.

Nováček, P. and Mederly, P. (2002) *Global Partnership for Development, Sustainable Development Index*, Olomouc, Czech Republic: Palacky University (for: American Council for the United Nations University).

Odum, E.P. (1971) *Fundamentals of Ecology*, Philadelphia: Saunders.

Odum, E.P. and Odum, H.T. (1953/1971) *Fundamentals of Ecology*, 3rd edn, Philadelphia: Saunders.

Odum, H.T. (1996) *Environmental Accounting, Emergy and Decision Making*, New York: Wiley.

———— (2002) 'Emergy accounting', in P. Bartelmus, *Unveiling Wealth – on Money, Quality of Life and Sustainability*, Dordrecht: Kluwer.

Opschoor, H. and van der Straaten, J. (1993) 'Sustainable development: an institutional approach', *Ecological Economics*, 7: 203–22.

Organization for Economic Co-operation and Development (OECD) (1989), *Economic Instruments for Environmental Protection*, Paris: OECD.

—— (1993) *Core Set of Indicators for Environmental Performance Reviews*, Environmental Monograph No. 83, Paris: OECD.

—— (2002) *Indicators to Measure Decoupling of Environmental Pressure from Economic Growth* (SG/SD(2002)1/FINAL) Paris: OECD. <http://www.oecd.org/officialdocuments/displaydocumentpdf/?cote=sg/sd(2002)1/final&doclanguage=en> (accessed 19 July 2011).

—— (2003) *OECD Environmental Indicators – Development, Measurement and Use* (Reference Paper). <http://www.oecd.org/dataoecd/7/47/24993546.pdf> (accessed 19 July 2011).

—— (2008) *Measuring Material Flows and Resource Productivity*, Synthesis Report, Paris: OECD. <http://www.oecd.org/dataoecd/55/12/40464014.pdf> (accessed 2 March 2012).

—— (2011) 'The green growth strategy, reshaping the OECD's work agenda for the years to come'. <http://www.oecd.org/dataoecd/62/59/48302542.pdf> (accessed 21 July 2011).

Osborn, D. and Bigg, T. (1998) *Earth Summit II, Outcomes and Analysis*, London: Earthscan.

Paterson, C. (2008) 'The concept of maximum sustainable yield and its limitations'. <http://www.unepscs.org/Refugia_Training/Fisheries%20Management%20Principles%20and%20Concepts/03-Concept-Maximum-Sustainable-Yield-Fisheries-Asia.pdf> (accessed 29 June 2011).

Perrings, C. (1995) 'Ecology, economics and ecological economics.', *Ambio*, 24: 60–3.

—— (2006) 'Resilience and sustainable development', *Environment and Development Economics*, 11: 417–27.

Pezzey, J. (1989) 'Economic Analysis of Sustainable Growth and Sustainable Development', Environment Department Working Paper No. 15, Washington, DC: World Bank.

Pigou, A.C. (1920/1932), *The Economics of Welfare.* London: Macmillan.

Prescott-Allen, R. (2001). *The Wellbeing of Nations: a Country-by-country Index of Quality of Life and the Environment*. Washington, DC: Island Press.

Quesnay, F. (1759/1972) 'The "Third Edition" of the *Tableau Economique*', in M. Kuczynski and R.L. Meek (eds), *Quesnay's Tableau Economique* (facsimile reproduction and English translation), London: Macmillan; reprinted in P. Bartelmus and E.K. Seifert (eds) (2003) *Green Accounting*, Aldershot: Ashgate.

Rennings, K., Koschel, H., Brockmann K.L. and Kühn, I. (1999) 'A regulatory framework for a policy of sustainability: lessons from the neo-liberal school.', *Ecological Economics*, 28: 197–212.

Ricardo, D. (1817/1963) *The Principles of Political Economy and Taxation*, Homewood, IL: Irwin.

Rodrik, D. (1997) *Has Globalization Gone Too Far?*, Washington, DC: Institute for International Economics.

Røpke, IL. (2005) 'Trends in the development of ecological economics from the late 1980s to the early 2000s', *Ecological Economics* 55: 262–90.

Sachs, I. (1976) 'Environment and styles of development', in: W.H. Matthews (ed.) *Outer Limits and Human Needs*, Uppsala: Dag Hammarskjöld Foundation.

—— (1980) *Stratégies de l'Ecodéveloppement* [Strategies of eco-development], Paris: Editions Ouvrières.

Sachs, W. (1995) 'From efficiency to sufficiency', *Resurgence*, 171: 6–8.

Sachs, W., Loske, R. and Linz, M. (1998) *Greening the North, Post-industrial Blueprint for Ecology and Equity*, London: Zed Books.

Samuelson, P.A. and Nordhaus, W.D. (1992) *Economics*, 14th edn, New York: McGraw-Hill.

Segal, J.M. (1999) *Graceful Simplicity, Towards a Philosophy and Politics of Simple Living*, New York: Holt.

Simonis, U. (2005) 'Global environmental governance: why we need a World Environmental Organisation', in G. Allan and M. Allshouse (eds) *Nature, Truth, and Value – Exploring the Thinking of Frederick Ferré*, Lanham, MD: Lexington Books.

Slesser, M. (1975) 'Accounting for energy', *Nature*, 254: 170–2.

Söderbaum, P. (1999) 'Values, ideology and politics in ecological economics', *Ecological Economics*, 28: 161–70.

—— (2008) *Understanding Sustainability Economics*, London and Sterling, VA: Earthscan.

Solow, R.M. (1974) 'The Economics of Resources or the Resources of Economics', *American Economic Review*, 64: 1–14.

Speth, J.G. (ed.) (2003) *Worlds Apart, Globalization and the Environment*, Washington, DC: Island Press.

Stahmer, C., Kuhn, M. and Braun, N. (1998) 'Physical Input–output Tables for Germany, 1990', Eurostat Working Papers No. 2/1998/B/1, European Commission.

Stakeholder Forum for a Sustainable Future (n.d.) 'Earthsummit 2012'. <http://www.earthsummit2012.org/> (accessed 15 July 2011).

Stavins, R.N., Wagner, A.F. and Wagner, G. (2003) 'Interpreting sustainability in economic terms: dynamic efficiency plus intergenerational equity', *Economic Letters*, 79: 339–43.

Stern, N. (2006) *The Economics of Climate Change: the Stern Review*, commissioned by the UK Treasury. <http://www.hm-treasury.gov.uk/sternreview_index.htm> (accessed 19 July 2011).

Steurer, A. (1992) *Stoffstrombilanz Österreich 1988* [Material flow balance Austria 1988], Schriftenreihe Soziale Ökologie, Vol. 26. Vienna.

Stiglitz, J.E., Sen, A. and Fitoussi, J.P. (2010). *Mismeasuring Our Lives, Why the GDP Doesn't Add Up*, New York and London: New Press.

Sustainable Europe Research Institute with Wuppertal Institute for Climate, Environment, Energy (2011) 'www.materialflows.net, the online portal for material flow data'. <http://www.materialflows.net/> (accessed 16 August 2011).

Svendsen, G.T. and Svendsen, G.L. (eds) (2009) *Handbook of Social Capital, the Troika of Sociology, Political Science and Economics*, Cheltenham and Northampton, MA: Edward Elgar.

Szargut, J. (2005) *Exergy Method, Technical and Ecological Applications*, Southampton and Boston: WIT Press.

Talberth, J. (2010) 'Measuring what matters: GDP, ecosystems and the environment'. <http://www.wri.org/stories/2010/04/measuring-what-matters-gdp-ecosystems-and environment> (accessed 19 July 2011).

Talberth, J., Cobb, C. and Slattery, N. (2007) *The Genuine Progress Indicator 2006, a Tool for Sustainable Development*, Oakland, CA: Redefining Progress. <http://www.scribd.com/doc/3061355/Genuine-Progress-Indicator-2006> (accessed 21 June 2011).

Tietenberg, T. (2005) *Environmental and Natural Resource Economics*, 7th edn, Boston: Addison-Wesley.

Tolba, M.K. (ed.) (2001) *Our Fragile World, Challenges and Opportunities for Sustainable Development*, Oxford: Eolss Publishers.

Turner, R.K., Pearce, D. and Bateman, I. (1993) *Environmental Economics, an Elementary Introduction*, Baltimore: Johns Hopkins University Press.

United Nations (1984) *A Framework for the Development of Environment Statistics*, New York: United Nations (sales no. E.84.XVII.12).

—— (1993) *Integrated Environmental and Economic Accounting*, New York: United Nations (sales no. E.93.XVII.12).

—— (1994). *Earth Summit, Agenda 21, the United Nations Programme of Action from Rio*, New York: United Nations (sales no. E.93.I.11).

—— (1996) *Indicators of Sustainable Development, Frameworks and Methodologies*, New York: United Nations (sales no. E.96.II.A.16).

—— (2001) *Indicators of Sustainable Development: Guidelines and Methodologies*, New York: United Nations (sales no. E.01.II.A.6).

—— (2003) *Johannesburg Declaration on Sustainable Development and Plan of Implementation of the World Summit on Sustainable Development*, New York: United Nations.

—— (2010a) 'Resolution adopted by the General Assembly (A/RES/65/1), Keeping the promise: united to achieve the Millennium Development Goals'. <http://www.un.org/en/mdg/summit2010/pdf/outcome_documentN1051260.pdf> (accessed 21 August 2011).

—— (2010b) 'The Millennium Development Goals Report. <http://mdgs.un.org/unsd/mdg/Resources/Static/Data/2010%20Stat%20Annex.pdf> (accessed on 19 July 2011).

—— (2011a) 'Global Compact'. <http://www.unglobalcompact.org/AboutTheGC/index.html>, updated 30 April 2011 (accessed 19 July 2011).

—— (2011b) 'Rio+20, United Nations Conference on Sustainable Development'. <http://www.uncsd2012.org/rio20/index.php?menu=14> (accessed 15 July 2011).

United Nations Conference on the Human Environment (1972) *Development and Environment*, report and working papers of a panel of experts, Mouton: United Nations and Ecole Pratique des Hautes Etudes.

United Nations Department of Economic and Social Affairs (2002) 'Second local Agenda 21 survey', Background paper no. 15, submitted by the International Council for Local Environmental Initiatives (DESA/DSD/PC2/BP15).

—— (2009–2010) 'What is GAID?'. <http://www.un-gaid.org/About/WhatisGAID/tabid/892/Default.aspx> (accessed 19 July 2011).

United Nations Development Programme (UNDP) (2010) *Human Development Report, Statistical Tables*, Oxford: Oxford University Press. <http://hdr.undp. org/en/media/HDR_2010_EN_Tables_reprint.pdf (accessed 19 July 2011).

United Nations Educational, Scientific and Cultural Organization (UNESCO) (n.d.) 'Teaching and learning for a sustainable future, activity 2: Dimensions of sustainable development'. <http://www.unesco.org/education/tlsf/TLSF/theme_a/ mod02/uncom02t02.htm (accessed 19 June 2011).

United Nations Environment Programme (UNEP) (1975) 'The proposed programme' (UNEP/GC/30), Nairobi.

—— (2011a) *Decoupling Natural Resource Use and Environmental Impacts from Economic Growth*, a report of the Working Group on Decoupling to the International Resource Panel. <http://www.unep.org/resourcepanel/decoupling/files/ pdf/Decoupling_Report_English.pdf> (accessed 12 July 2011).

—— (2011b) *Towards a Green Economy, Pathways to Sustainable Development and Poverty Eradication*. <http://www.unep.org/greeneconomy/GreenEconomy Report/tabid/29846/Default.aspx> (accessed 20 July 2011).

United Nations, European Commission, International Monetary Fund, Organisation for Economic Co-operation and Development and World Bank (2003) *Integrated Environmental and Economic Accounting 2003*, final draft circulated for information prior to official editing. <http://unstats.un.org/unsd/envaccounting/seea. asp> (accessed 20 July 2011).

United Nations Framework Convention on Climate Change (UNFCCC) (n.d.). <http://unfccc.int/essential_background/convention/items/2627.php> (accessed 20 July 2011).

United Nations Procurement Division (2004) 'The Global Compact'. <http://www. un.org/Depts/ptd/global.htm> (accessed on 19 June 2011).

United Nations Statistics Division (2010) 'UNSD environmental indicators'. <http://unstats.un.org/unsd/ENVIRONMENT/qindicators.htm> (accessed 28 June 2011).

Uno, K. and Bartelmus, P. (eds) (1998) *Environmental Accounting in Theory and Practice*, Dordrecht: Kluwer.

US Department of the Interior (2010) 'How should adaptive management be implemented?'. <http://www.doi.gov/initiatives/AdaptiveManagement/howto.html> (accessed 20 July 2011).

US National Weather Service, JetStream – online school for weather (2010) 'The earth-atmosphere energy balance'. <http://www.srh.noaa.gov/jetstream//atmos/ energy.htm> (accessed 28 June 2011).

Veblen, T. (1899/1967) *The Theory of the Leisure Class*, New York: Macmillan.

von Carlowitz, H.C. (1713) *Sylvicultura Oeconomica* [Economic forestry], Leipzig: Braun.

von Weizsäcker, E.U., Lovins, A. and Lovins, H. (1997) *Factor Four: Doubling Wealth, Halving Resource Use*, London: Earthscan.

Wall, G. (2008) 'Exergy', in C.J. Cleveland (ed.) *Encyclopedia of Earth*. <http:// www.eoearth.org/article/Exergy> (accessed 20 July 2011).

Weitzman, M.L. (2009) 'On modelling and interpreting the economics of catastrophic climate change', *Review of Economics and Statistics*, 91: 1–19.

Welfens, P. (2012) 'Atomstromkosten und -risiken: Haftpflichtfragen und Optionen rationaler Wirtschaftspolitik' [Cost and risk of nuclear energy: liability problems and options of rational energy policy], Discussion Paper 191, Wuppertal, Germany: European Institute for International Economic Relations. <http://www. eiiw.eu/fileadmin/eiiw/Daten/Sonstiges/bookenergie2011paper.pdf> (accessed 3 March 2012).

White, L. (1967) 'The historical roots of our ecological crisis', *Science*, 155: 1203–7.

World Bank (2003a) *ICT for Development, Contributing to the Millennium Development Goals*, Washington, DC: World Bank. <www.infodev.org/en/ Document.19.pdf> (accessed 14 July 2011).

—— (2003b). *World Development Report 2003, Sustainable Development in a Dynamic World, Transforming Institutions, Growth, and Quality of Life*, New York: Oxford University Press.

—— (2006) *Where is the Wealth of Nations? Measuring Capital for the 21st Century*, Washington, DC: World Bank.

—— (2011) *World Development Indicators 2011*, Washington DC: World Bank. <http://data.worldbank.org/data-catalog/world-development-indicators?cid= GPD_WDI> (accessed 18 July 2011).

World Business Council for Sustainable Development (WBCSD) (n.d.) 'Business solutions for a sustainable world'. <http://www.wbcsd.org/home.aspx> (accessed 3 March 2012).

World Commission on Environment and Development (WCED) (1987) *Our Common Future*, Oxford: Oxford University Press.

World Trade Organization (WTO) (n.d.) (a) 'The Doha agenda'. <http://www.wto. org/english/thewto_e/whatis_e/tif_e/doha1_e.htm> (accessed 19 June 2011).

—— (b) 'The environment: a specific concern'. <http://www.wto.org/english/ thewto_e/whatis_e/tif_e/bey2_e.htm> (accessed 19 June 2011).

—— (c) 'Uruguay Round Agreement, Marrakesh Agreement Establishing the World Trade Organization'. <http://www.wto.org/english/docs_e/legal_e/04- wto_e.htm> (accessed 19 June 2011).

World Wide Fund for Nature, Zoological Society of London and Global Footprint Network (2010) *Living Planet Report 2010, Biodiversity, Biocapacity and Development*,Gland: WWF. <http://assets.panda.org/downloads/lpr2010.pdf> (accessed 25 July 2011).

Yale Center for Environmental Law and Policy and Center for International Earth Science Information Network (1997–2006) *Environmental Sustainability Index 2002, 2005, Environmental Performance Index 2006*. <http://sedac.ciesin. columbia.edu/es/esi/downloads.html> (accessed 20 July 2011).

Zero Emissions Research and Initiative (2011) 'What is ZERI'. <http://www.zeri. org/ZERI/About_ZERI.html> (accessed 19 June 2011).

Author index

Arrow, K. 83
Atkinson, G. 9
AtKisson, A 69
Auty, R.M. 83
Ayres, R.U. 9

Barbier, E.B. 78
Bartelmus, P. 5, 8, 14, 40, 64, 66, 67, 68, 70, 92, 94, 106
Bebbington, J. 45
Beckerman, W. 8, 36, 101
Bhagwati, J, 107
Bigg, T. 117
Bishop, R.C. 44
Böhringer, C. 106
Brand, F. 34, 35
Braungart, M. 45
Bringezu, S. 18, 19, 21, 40
Brown, L.R. 13
Brown, M.T. 22, 24
BUND 117

Carson, R. 8
Castiglione, D. 71
Center for International Earth Science Information Network 102, 106
Centre for Bhutan Studies 69
Chertow, M.R. 45
Ciriacy-Wantrup, S.V. 44
Coastal Service Center, NOAA 26
Cobb, C. 62, 63, 69
Cole, H.S.D. 36
Commission of the European Communities *see* European Union
Conrad, K. 82

Cortright, J. 84
Costanza, R. 8, 19, 26, 57
Crook, C. 45
Crowards, T.M. 44

Daly, H.E. 4, 8, 24, 26, 37, 40, 62, 82, 100, 107
Dasgupta, P. 82, 83
de Groot, R. 34, 35
de Haan, M. 89
Diamond, J. 13
Dixon, J.A. 74
Dorfman, R. 94
Dubner, S.J. xiii
Dziegielewska, D. 59

Economist, The 73, 82, 107
Ehrenfeld 45
Ehrlich, P.R. 4, 8
Ekins, P. 35, 105
Elliot, R. 44
Elliot, S. 84
European Association for Bioeconomic Studies (E.A.B.S) 9
European Commission *see* European Union
European Environment Agency 21
European Union (EU) 39, 40, 45, 69, 71, 84
Eurostat 18, 21
Ewing, B. 16, 17

Faber, M. 44
Factor 10 Club 40
Farley, J. 100

140   *Author index*

Faucheux, S. 100
Federal Government, Germany 110, 111, 116
Frank, R.H. 41
Funtowicz, S.O. 40, 82

Gallup 69, 110
Georgescu-Roegen, N. 21
Gore, A. 8, 13
Goulder, I.H. 77
Gray, R. 45
Grossman, G.M. 78

Haeckel, E. 1
Hanley, N. 8, 101
Hardin, G. 35
Hepburn, C. 60
Hicks, J.R. xiii, 64
Hinterberger, F. 40
Hoekstra, R. 93
Holdren, J.P. 4
Holling, C.S. 38
Hotelling, H. 83
Howell, S.L. 66
Huber, J. 45

Intergovernmental Panel on Climate Change (IPCC) 15, 16, 57, 78
International Labour Organizations (ILO) 98
International Organization for Standardization (ISO) 71
IUCN (World Conservation Union) 40, 105
Islam, S.M.N. 80

Jevons, W.S. 42
Jochem, P.E.P. 106

Kates, R.W. 115
Kee, P. 89
Kokkelenberg, E.C. 66
Koopmans, T.C. 80
Klitgaard, K. 101
Krall, L. 101
Krueger, A.B. 78
Kuznets, S. 78

Landefeld, J.S. 66
Lange, G.-M. 82

Lawn, P. 8, 37, 108
Leipert, C. 62
Leontief, W. 93
Levitt, S.D. xiii
Lomborg, B. 8
Lovelock, J. E. 8, 9

McDonough, W. 45
Mäler, K.-G. 83
Malthus, T. 8
Mander, J. 107, 110, 113
Martinez-Alier, J. 116
Max-Neef, M. 62, 69, 98
Meadows, D. 30, 35, 36, 38, 40
Mederly, P. 102, 106
Meyer, B. 28, 29, 90
Millennium Ecosystem Assessment 34
Munasinghe, M. 84
Murray, J. 93

Netherlands Environmental Assessment Agency 111
Newsweek 84
Nordhaus, W.D. 8, 36, 56, 61, 62, 66, 76, 79, 80, 82, 84, 101
Norgaard, R.B. 9
Nováček, P. 102, 106

Odum, E.P. 34
Odum, H.T. 22
Opschoor, H. 105
Organisation for Economic Co-operation and Development (OECD) 21, 39, 40, 75, 122
Osborn, D. 117

Paterson, C. 35
Perrings, C. 25
Pezzey, J. 61
Pigou, A.C. 51, 76
Prescott-Allen, R. 102, 106

Ravetz, J.R. 40, 82
Rennings, K. 44, 105
Rodrik, D. 107
Røpke, I. 9, 14

Sachs, W. 7, 41
Sachs, I. 109
Samuelson, P.A. 82, 101

Segal, J.M. 41
Simon, J.L. 8
Simonis, U. 113
Slesser, M. 19
Söderbaum, P. 8, 100
Solow, R.M. 83
Speth, J.G. 106
Stahmer, C. 88
Stakeholder Forum for a Sustainable
   Future 118
Stern, N. 55, 56, 79
Steurer, A. 21
Stiglitz, J.E. 69
Sustainable Europe Research Institute
   (SERI) 21
Svendsen, G.L. 71
Svendsen, G.T. 71
Szargut, J. 21

Talberth, J. 62, 69
Tietenberg, T. 8, 83, 101
Time 84
Tobin, J. 61, 62
Tolba, M.K. 21
Turner, R.K. 8, 35, 101

Ulgiati, S. 22, 24
United Nations 21, 31, 38, 44, 45, 66,
   75, 84, 99, 105, 111, 118; Conference
   on the Human Environment 117;
   Department of Economic and
   Social Affairs 116; Development
   Programme (UNDP) 28, 99, 106;
   Educational Scientific and Cultural
   Organization (UNESCO) 100;

Environment Programme (UNEP)
   39, 84, 109, 122; Procurement
   Division 45; Statistics Division
   (UNSD) 15
U.S. Department of the Interior 38
U.S. National Weather Service 20

van den Bergh, J.C.J.M. 93
van der Straaten, J. 105
Veblen, T. 41
von Carlowitz, H.C. 105
von Weizsäcker, E.U. 28, 42

Wall, G. 21
Weitzman, M.L. 79, 80
Welfens, P. 55
White, L. 9
Wilde, O. 49
Wood, R. 93
World Bank 29, 71, 84, 122
World Business Council for Sustainable
   Development (WBCSD) 41
World Commission on Environment
   and Development (WCED) 99,
   100, 117
World Conservation Union *see* IUCN
World Trade Organization (WTO) 106
World Wide Fund for Nature (WWF)
   30, 38

Yale Center for Environmental Law
   and Policy 102, 106

Zero Emission Research Initiative
   (ZERI) 45

Subject index

activity analysis *see* linear programming
adaptive management 38
Africa 17, 66, 68, 99
Agenda 21 112, 117; local 109, 116
anthropocentric view of the environment 2, 86
Asia 17
Australia 15

basic human needs *see* human needs, basic
Bhutan 69
biocapacity 16–18, 23, 30
bioeconomics 9
biomimicry 45
Botswana 82

capital 26, 64; consumption 63–4, 65, 66; maintenance 65, 69, 80, 121; natural *see* natural capital; produced 65, 66; widening 62
capitalism 102, 113, 117
carbon: price 56, 76; tax 56, 76, 90
carrying capacity 4, 25, 30, 105, 109, 120
China 15, 17, 66, 68
civil society 52, 117, 118
climate change 8, 13, 14–16, 111; cost 55–7, 76, 78; discounting 55, 79; Framework Convention 117; policy 76, 79, 90
co-evolutionary economics 9, 100

command and control *see* rules and regulations
commodification of nature 24; *see also* nature, value
comparative advantage 103
computable general equilibrium 75, 82–3, 90–1
conspicuous consumption *see* overconsumption
consumer surplus 53, 59
corporate environmental accounting 64–5, 69, 71
corporate social responsibility 41, 42, 45
cost–benefit analysis 8, 52, 74
cradle-to-cradle design 45
critical natural capital 26, 34–5, 102

decoupling of environmental impact from economic growth 39, 40
deep ecologists 2, 5, 6, 13
defensive expenditure 62
deglobalization 113, 114 *see also* localization
delinking *see* decoupling
dematerialization 39, 40, 84, 90
demographic growth 4, 8, 35
demographic policy 38, 49
developing countries 81, 98
development 97–8, 100, 123 *see also* sustainable development; indices 105–6; local *see* eco-development
Development Decades *see* International Development Strategies

digital revolution *see* information and communication technology
discounting 54–5, 60, 79, 80, 91; social 54–5, 60, 79, 83
discovery *see* natural resource, discovery
Doha negotiations 106, 114
double dividend 77

earth: Charter 44; summits 111–12, 117–18
eco-centric view of the environment 2, 86
eco-development 109–10, 116
eco-efficiency 40, 42
eco-tax 76, 77, 90 *see also* carbon, tax
eco-techniques 109, 110
eco-nomics 5, 6, 8; history 6–7, 125
ecological deficit/credit 16–17, 18
ecological economics 5, 6, 8, 14, 24, 43–4, 100, 101 *see also* environmental-economic polarization
Ecological Footprint 16–18, 23, 30–1
ecological management rules 37–8
ecological sustainability *see* sustainability, ecological
ecological tax reform 76–7
ecology 1, 6, 9
economic agents 2, 70; environmental effects 50–1
economic growth 62, 63, 97, 98, 103, 104 *see also* decoupling *and* environmental Kuznets curve; green 122; limits 4, 80; models 91; sustainable 66, 68, 78–9, 80, 83–4, 122, 123
economic indicators 70, 88; greening 65, 70, 122
economic sustainability *see* sustainability, economic
economic value *see* valuation, economic
economics: institutional 101; laissez-faire 9, 78; mainstream 4, 6, 101
economy 2, 3; black-box 3, 14, 19, 87; green *see* green economy; new 84
ecosystem 34; accounts 71; equilibrium 25, 34; management 38; resilience 25, 34, 44; services 2–3, 25, 34, 57, 58–9

emergy 21–2
Emission Trading System 76
energy: accounts 19, 21; conservation 18, 21; global balance 19–20; theory of value 19, 24
environment 1–2
environmental accounts *see* System for integrated Environmental and Economic Accounting *and* corporate environmental accounting
environmental assets *see* natural capital
environmental cost 40, 63, 65, 66, 71 *see also* social cost; internalization 8, 74–5; marginal 40, 58–9, 76, 77
environmental degradation 14, 68, 71
environmental disaster 4, 8, 13–14, 28, 30, 35–6, 55
environmental economics 5, 6, 7, 8, 50, 74–5 *see also* environmental-economic polarization
environmental education 75, 109
environmental ethics 41, 44, 54
environmental externalities 50–1, 52, 58; internalization *see* environmental cost, internalization
environmental functions *see* ecosystem, services
environmental impact 4, 69, 82 *see also* environmental pressure
environmental indicators 14, 15, 21
environmental Kuznets curve 78, 79
environmental limits 4, 40, 49, 91–2, 94
Environmental Management and Audit Scheme 71
environmental policy 40, 41, 78; instruments 75–6
environmental pressure 6, 16, 21
environmental protection 74 *see also* defensive expenditure
environmental services *see* ecosystem, services
environmental standards 32, 33–4, 59, 101, 122 *see also* safe minimum standards *and* environmental limits
environmental sustainability *see* sustainability, environmental
Environmental Sustainability Index 102, 106
environmental targets *see* environmental standards

environmental-economic polarization
6, 7, 26–7, 49–50, 86–7, 113, 120
environmental-economic reconciliation
87, 91–3, 100, 122
environmentally adjusted net capital
formation (ECF) 65, 66, 68, 70
environmentally adjusted net domestic
product (EDP) 65, 66, 70
equilibrium: economic 8, 58, 75 *see
also* computable general equilibrium;
temperature 20
equity: inter-generational 44, 100
see also discounting, social;
international 100; intra-generational
44, 100
Europe 99, 103
European Union 18, 19, 40, 71, 76, 84,
97
exergy 19, 21
externalities *see* environmental
externalities

factors of natural resource productivity
28, 39, 40, 42
feasibility space 91, 92
fiscal (dis)incentives *see* market,
instruments
full world 4, 5

Gaia hypothesis 8, 9, 13
general equilibrium *see* equilibrium,
economic
Genuine Progress Indicator (GPI) 62–3
Germany 15, 28, 29, 66, 67, 76–7, 88,
110–11, 116–17
Global Compact 114, 115, 118
global governance 111–13
global warming *see* climate change
globalization 103–4, 106–7, 113;
sustainability effects 102–4, 107, 113
good life 41, 102
green accounting *see* System for
integrated Environmental and
Economic Accounting
green economy 38, 84, 121
greenhouse gases 19, 20
gross domestic product (GDP) 61, 62,
66, 70; bashing 63, 69; green 65;
physical 88
Gross National Happiness 69

happiness 69
hidden material flows 18
homo oeconomicus 44
Hotelling rule 83
human capital 64, 66, 71
Human Development Index 28, 98–9, 106
human needs 25, 98, 100, 121; basic
38, 91, 98
hybrid accounts 87, 88–9
hybrid models 90

income 2, 64; distribution 70, 78, 100;
maximization 5, 78; national 70;
sustainability 64
Indicator of Sustainable Economic
Welfare 62
industrial ecology 9
industrialized countries 18, 39, 66, 113
information and communication
technology 84, 107
input–output model 28, 29, 81, 90, 93
input–output table 81, 87, 89, 93;
physical 88
integration *see* policy integration
interaction of environment and
economy 2–4, 24, 64
inter-generational equity *see* equity,
inter-generational
International Development Strategies
99, 104–5, 114
invisible hand *see* market
IPAT equation 4
irreversibility of environmental impacts
26, 44
ISO 14000 71

Japan 18

Latin America 17
limits to growth report 8, 28, 30, 35–6, 38
linear programming 91–2, 93–4
Living Planet Index 38
lobbying 52, 66, 74
localization 113

maintenance cost 63, 65, 120
market 6, 40, 73, 83; failure 40, 51–2,
58, 73, 82; instruments 75–6, 123;
price 50, 53, 58–9 *see also* valuation,
economic

material flow accounts 18–19, 20, 21, 27–8
maximum sustainable yield 26, 35
metabolic consistency 42, 45
micro–macro analysis 6, 120–1
Millennium Development Goals 31–2, 105, 114
modelling 28–31, 80, 90–1; climate change 56–7
multi-lateral environmental agreements 114

Namibia 82
National Accounting Matrix including Environmental Accounts 88–9
national accounts *see* System of National Accounts
natural capital 63, 64, 83 *see also* critical natural capital; consumption 63–4, 65, 70; value 54, 60
natural disaster *see* environmental disaster
natural growth 35
natural resource: curse 81, 83; depletion 35, 63, 70 *see also* tragedy of the commons; discovery 26; economics 83; productivity 28, 40, 42; rent 60, 83; rent capture 81, 82
natural resources 2, 3, 20; common property *see* natural resources, open-access; exhaustible 26, 77, 83; non-renewable *see* natural resources, exhaustible; open-access 35; renewable 26
nature 2–3, 45, 108–9; services *see* ecosystem, services; value 24, 44, 49, 50, 53–4
net domestic product 70; green *see* environmentally adjusted net domestic product
Netherlands 110, 111
new growth theory *see* economy, new
non-governmental organizations 110–11, 113, 116–17
non-sustainability 14, 23, 28
North America 99
nuclear accident 55; social cost 79

Oceania 17, 99
optimal extraction 77, 83
overconsumption 41, 50–1

Pareto optimality 58
Philippines 74
polarization *see* environmental-economic polarization
policy integration 44, 99, 108
polluter-pays-principle 75
population growth *see* demographic growth
poverty 58, 84, 111, 117
precautionary principle 38
pressure-state-response framework 21
producer surplus 60
public goods/bads 51–2, 73
public–private partnership 45, 111, 117, 118

quality of life 25, 69

rebound effects 42
residuals 18, 88
resource economics *see* natural resource, economics
resource curse *see* natural resource, curse
resource productivity *see* natural resource, productivity
Rio: Declaration 44; +20 see earth, summits
rules and regulations 43, 44, 75, 123

safe minimum standards 25, 38, 44, 105
scarcity 50, 52, 58
Simon–Ehrlich wager 8
social capital 64, 66, 71
social cost 76, 77, 103
social justice *see* equity
source and sink functions *see* ecosystem, services
South Africa 15
Southern Africa 81
substitution *see* sustainability, strong/weak
sufficiency 40, 41
sustainability 69, 87, 119, 120–1; ecological 25, 30–1; economic 61, 65, 121, 122; environmental 7, 31–2, 65; financial 1; maximum 14, 35; strong/weak 26–7, 65–6, 68, 101–2
sustainability economics 4–5, 8, 115–16, 124
sustainability indicators 14, 19, 21, 30, 32, 121–2

sustainability models 33, 78–9, 80, 83–4, 91–2
sustainability policy 38–40, 110–11, 123 sustainability science 115
sustainability targets 28, 31–2, 33–4, 122
sustainable development 97–101, 105, 115, 116; conferences *see* earth, summits; definition 100; dimensions 99–100; indicators 21, 102, 103; indices 102, 106; pillars *see* sustainable development, dimensions; policies 108, 110–11, 117, 123
Sweden 18
System for integrated Environmental and Economic Accounting (SEEA) 63–4, 68–9, 122; case studies 66–8; indicators 65, 66–8, 70; revision 66, 70–1; valuations 68, 70
System of National Accounts (SNA) 63, 69–70, 80

technology 28, 42, 80, 81, 84 *see also* information and communications technology
threshold hypothesis 62
throughput 40
total economic value 53–4, 59
Total Material Requirement 18, 88
trade liberalization 103, 104, 106
tragedy of the commons 26, 35

uncertainty 38, 44, 54, 79, 124
United Arab Emirates 17
United Kingdom 18, 42
United Nations: Commission on Sustainable Development 112; Environment Programme 39, 109, 112–13
USA 15, 17, 62, 66, 69, 110
utility 4, 58; maximization 24, 80, 82; measurement 52, 57, 121

vacuum economics 82
valuation: cost–benefit 52–3; economic 52–4, 60, 123; energy 19, 22, 24; human bias 14, 24, 49, 50

well-being *see* utility *and* welfare
Well-Being Index 102, 106
welfare 4, 53, 100; function 83; maximization 5, 58, 83, 100; measure 28, 30, 61–3, 69; sustainable 61, 62, 91 *see also* sustainability, economic
willingness to pay 52, 53, 58, 59
World Commission on Environment and development 99, 100, 117
World Conservation Strategy 105
World Environment Organization 113
World Trade Organization (WTO) 97, 102, 106; greening 113–14

Appendix: Historical perspective of *eco*-nomics

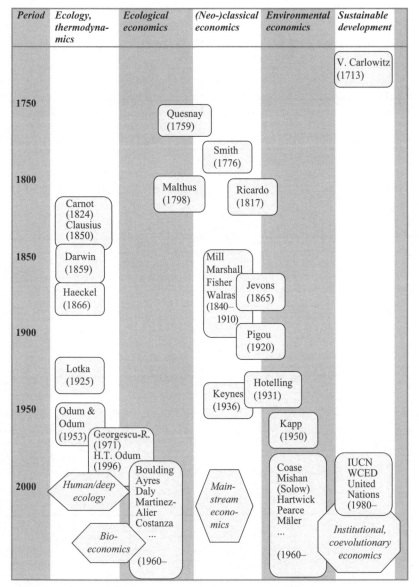

Period	Ecology, thermodynamics	Ecological economics	(Neo-)classical economics	Environmental economics	Sustainable development
					V. Carlowitz (1713)
1750			Quesnay (1759)		
			Smith (1776)		
1800		Malthus (1798)	Ricardo (1817)		
	Carnot (1824) Clausius (1850)				
1850	Darwin (1859)		Mill Marshall Fisher Walras (1840–1910)	Jevons (1865)	
	Haeckel (1866)				
1900			Pigou (1920)		
	Lotka (1925)				
			Keynes (1936)	Hotelling (1931)	
1950	Odum & Odum (1953)	Georgescu-R. (1971) H.T. Odum (1996)		Kapp (1950)	
2000	*Human/deep ecology*	Boulding Ayres Daly Martinez-Alier Costanza ...	*Mainstream economics*	Coase Mishan (Solow) Hartwick Pearce Mäler ...	IUCN WCED United Nations (1980–
		Bioeconomics (1960–		(1960–	*Institutional, coevolutionary economics*

Source: Bartelmus (2008: Plate 2.1), with kind permission from Springer Science+Business Media B.V.